# HOW
# BRANDS
# BLOW

**A** *...Gasp!* **BOOK**
**GASP FOUR LTD.**
**GREAT BRITAIN**
**Gasp. Agency**

First published in 2023
Copyright © Ryan Wallman & Giles Edwards *(...Gasp!)*

# CLOWNS TO THE LEFT OF ME JOKERS TO THE RIGHT

'A sober and hilarious indictment of the advertising and marketing world, where you will find your greatest frustrations and your own professional sins. Be ready to hold up a mirror.'

**CHRISTINA GARNETT**

◇◇◇◇◇◇◇

'This remarkable book has already had a profound effect on my long career in advertising...*I'M LEAVING!*'

**MARK DENTON**

◇◇◇◇◇◇◇

'Not only is How Brands Blow visually in your face, it's also violently prodding your gooey brain and challenging conventional 'yawn' marketing tactics. Packed with short snappy snippets of goodness, delivered with wry humour and simple smarts – it's a must read for all marketing humans.

Trigger warning: Coulrophobic humans beware!'

**KATE TOON**

'I don't believe Edwards and Wallman wrote this book at all. It could only have been plucked from the tormented souls of everyone in the marketing world who's ever slapped their brow in despair and/ or disbelief. For them to turn our pain into something so enormously funny is a truly wicked thing to do.'

**ANDREW BOULTON**

◇◇◇◇◇◇◇

'I think Depends should sponsor this book as pant-wetting poses a serious risk to the unprepared in-public reader.'

**LISL MACDONALD**

◇◇◇◇◇◇◇

'I'd buy this book just for the brilliant art direction. The writing had me laughing and crying: laughing at how true it is and crying at how true it is.'

**DAVE TROTT**

'Hilarious, hard-hitting and a hell of a way to learn to do better in the mess we've made of branding, marketing and advertising. Read it and weep - you will weep because you'll see yourself somewhere in all this and wish you hadn't.'

## VIKKI ROSS

◇◇◇◇◇◇◇

'There is no doubt that this is THE masterwork of recent times and a vital new addition to the laboratory of marketing science. 'How Brands Blow' disrupted me at a most fundamental level. Its advanced combination of purpose, agility and incredibly artificial intelligence makes this a book every marketer should buy, fail to understand and then quote endlessly in meetings and on the bus home to random commuters.'

## MARK RITSON

'The second album is always the trickiest. You have your whole life to write the first, then only a couple of years to write the follow up.

Luckily, Ryan Wallman and Giles Edwards have made The Bends rather than Use Your Illusion. How Brands Blow is everything you want it to be, and much more. Building on Delusions of Brandeur, finding fresh ways to eviscerate the pomposity of adland, it will make you howl with laughter and pain - the truth cuts deep. So, put down that Metaverse strategy, How Brands Blow is everything every marketer needs to read right now.'

## NICK ELLIS

◇◇◇◇◇◇◇

'A funny, insightful and beautiful book that is worth buying just to keep your spirits up as you head to your next client meeting in Milton Keynes.'

## ROB MAYHEW

CON
MEN
IN
TENTS

CHAPTER

MARKETING

**DO THE DATA CONFIRM WHAT YOU THINK?**

**YES**

**THE DATA ARE ACCURATE**

**NO**

**THE DATA ARE SPURIOUS**

# A SIMPLE SOLUTION TO A COMPLICATED PROBLEM

The way that some marketers talk about marketing,
you'd think it was more complex than neurosurgery.

There is endless industry talk about automation, platforms, CRM, AI, AR, VR, ad tech, martech, machine learning, blockchain – the list goes on.

But in my opinion, all this stuff is at best peripheral and at worst irrelevant to the core function of marketing. In many cases, these tactics and tech-tics serve to make marketing far more complicated than it need be.

Much as it might threaten our collective ego to admit it, the truth is that marketing isn't rocket science (and indeed some people argue that it isn't a science at all). This is not to suggest that it's easy – or that there's no merit in newer technologies – but the fundamental principles of marketing are relatively simple.

Mark Ritson captured this point beautifully in his series of Effies campaign case studies.

According to Mark, the 'perfectly effective' marketing campaign is characterised by nine elements:

- Diagnosis (qualitative and quantitative)
- Clear strategic objectives
- Long, mass-marketing branding
- Shorter, targeted performance
- Tight, differentiated positioning
- Heavy, consistent codification (i.e. use of distinctive brand assets)
- Greater investment than competitors
- Astonishing creativity
- Multiple integrated channels.

It's as simple (albeit difficult to execute) as that. If you care about effectiveness, which admittedly doesn't seem to be a given for some marketers, this list should be the reference point for all your marketing campaigns.

The problem, of course, is that it's not sexy (no offence, Mark). It doesn't involve any tech wizardry and it won't be talked about at all the cool conferences. It doesn't even include an acronym, FFS.

And that's why it won't appeal to everyone. As Dave Trott once said: 'complicated seems clever to stupid people'. But smart marketers will embrace the simplicity of Mark's approach, if they haven't already.

And that spells good news for those of us on the agency side, because 'astonishing creativity' is a crucial ingredient in the mix. Despite what some thought leaders and their thought disciples would have you believe, creativity can make a huge difference to the success of a campaign. It shouldn't be some afterthought, slapped on to the tactics like cheap cologne.

Rory Sutherland was recently asked what he considered to be the biggest challenge facing Ogilvy in the next 10 years. His typically frank response was:

'I think that the whole advertising industry has totally lost the plot. It has become obsessed with that part of advertising which is a media targeting and optimisation process.'

The obvious solution is for agencies to focus on making great creative work. Simple, really.

IT HAS BECOME OBSESSED WITH THAT PART OF ADVERTISING WHICH IS A MEDIA TARGETING AND OPTIMISATION PROCESS.

# HOW TO BE A MODERN MARKETING GURU

1. Share your 'insights'. For example, say that it's important to do stuff that people will like, rather than stuff that people will hate.

2. Blog about the value of blogging. And nothing else.

3. Use forced colloquial expressions a lot. It makes you seem edgy yet approachable.

4. Insist that traditional forms of marketing are dead. Do this in direct-mail pieces, long-copy whitepapers, 30-second videos – that sort of thing.

5. Quantity over quality. In fact, everything over quality.

6. Build a 'tribe' of like-minded, similarly deluded people.

7. Coin a catchy analogy about modern marketing. Something like: 'content is the manure; social media is the laxative'.

8. Wear the same colour of shirt at every event. This is bona fide marketing genius, apparently.

9. Understand that you are marketing one thing and one thing only. Yourself.

YOU NEED AN INFLUENCER CAMPAIGN.
TO GIVE YOUR MARKETING AUTHENTICITY.
OF COURSE NOT. COGNITIVE DISSONANCE IS DEAD!

Why did
Simon Sinek
cross the road?

1. Consumers would be simultaneously surprised and delighted at all times during the course of their everyday lives. Looking at a product label, being confronted by an online pop-up, reading a company's mission statement: all of these would evoke something close to ecstasy.

2. Nobody would ever choose a product for its functional purpose. People wouldn't even buy a paperclip until they knew the manufacturer's stance on the political situation in Chile and its views on the plight of the Madagascan tree frog.

3. People would be unfailingly loyal to the brands they love. As monogamous devotees, they would travel up hill and down dale to be with their chosen one, even if there were a perfectly good alternative left on the shelf (of their local 7−Eleven).

4. Everybody would cherish their interactions with chatbots − not just for their illusion of efficiency, but also for their robotic charm. Dealing with humans would be considered a tiresome ordeal.

5. Nobody would deal with any company that was not fully digitally transformed, or at the very least on an exciting journey of digital transformation. And only the most pathetic Luddite would buy a jar of jam or a loaf of bread that wasn't blockchain-authenticated.

6. People would adore being personally stalked by online advertising. After buying, say, a funeral service for a loved one, nothing would make them happier than spending the next three years seeing banner ads for coffins.

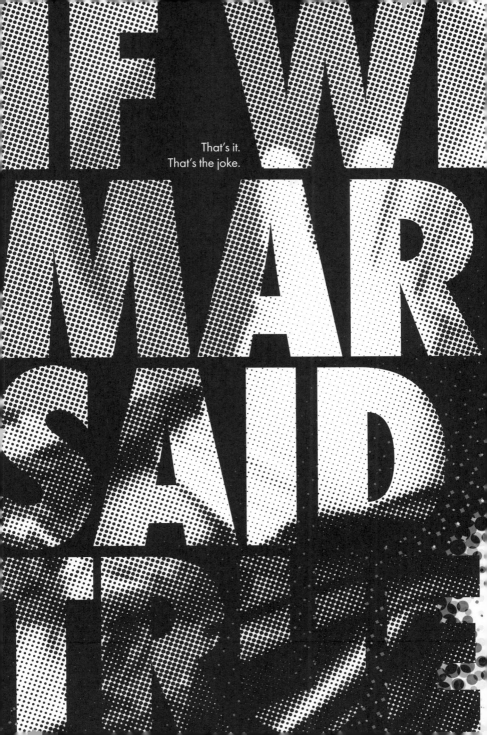

IF WE
MAR
SAID
IT TRUE

That's it.
That's the joke.

# THE INFLUENCER DICTIONARY

### Binfluencers
Seem to influence an awful lot of people but what they say is rubbish.
Most LinkedIn influencers are binfluencers.

### Finfluencers
Slippery characters who use fishy stories to build social media fame.

### Ginfluencers
People who believe they have influence when they are under the influence.
Ginfluencers typically post unsolicited life advice on Facebook.

### Kinfluencers
Those whose influence is limited to their immediate family.
Practically synonymous with 'thought leaders'.

### Sinfluencers
People who promote the teachings of Gary V.

### Skinfluencers
Superficial types who are especially prevalent on Instagram.
Sometimes accused of using their influence purely for monetary gain
(and where there's smoke, there's Fyre).

### Twinfluencers
Two influencers whose advice is so similar they might as well share
the same genetic material. Any two content marketing influencers
are twinfluencers.

# BRANDING   VS  MARKETING

Branding is landscape.

Marketing is portrait.

Branding is vegetable.

Marketing is mineral.

Branding is the superego.

Marketing is the id.

Branding defines culture.

Marketing defines denture.

Branding builds community.

Marketing builds a comfortable 2-bed apartment just off the highway.

Branding creates a mindset.

Marketing creates a mind-altering substance. We have notified the police.

Branding is the force that connects all life.

Marketing is Baby Yoda.

I had a Gary
Vee joke but
I crushed

# INFLUENCER EPIDEMIC

A particularly virulent strain of influencer, known as type Vee, is currently infecting large numbers of people around the world.

The virus is spread primarily via shouty videos, which social media users will find almost impossible to avoid.

Early symptoms of infection include compulsive repetition of the word 'hustle', an abnormal proclivity for exclamation marks, and a tendency for aggressive behaviour towards non-infected people. Later stages are characterised by a progressive decline in cognitive function, ultimately leading to incoherence.

People at particularly high risk of infection include gullible marketers, bitcoin bros, and those insufferable twats who introduce themselves as entrepreneurs at parties.

Sufferers are advised to get a grip.

# RUNNING THEIR OWN RACE: THE PROBLEM WITH DEMOGRAPHIC GENERALISATIONS

**W**hen I was a kid of about 7 or 8 years of age, I became borderline-obsessed with the movie Chariots of Fire.

If you know Chariots of Fire, I'll give you a minute to roll your eyes, because it probably seems like a ridiculously pretentious choice of entertainment for a young lad. It's a fair cop.

What can I say? I guess I was taken in by all the running, perhaps thinking I would one day become an Olympic champion (spoiler alert: I didn't quite make it).

But before long – or so I like to tell myself – I began to understand the real themes of Chariots of Fire. Let's just say it didn't win four Academy Awards for being a film about some blokes jogging along a beach.

Chariots of Fire is the mostly true story of two British men who competed at the 1924 Olympics. One, Eric Liddell, is a devout Christian who would later become a missionary in China. He sensationally refuses to run an Olympic heat on a Sunday – on account of it being the Sabbath – and therefore forfeits his favourite event, the 100 metres.

Eric Liddell literally believes that he runs for God. More figuratively speaking, he tells his supporters that faith will give them the power 'to see the race to its end' (one of many lines in the film that makes me well up, despite my avowed atheism – honestly, I implore you to watch that scene if you haven't seen it before).

The other protagonist, Harold Abrahams, is a Jewish man who is driven by resentment at being cast as an outsider by the British society of the time – and particularly by the anti-Semitism he encounters. As he later explained in a BBC interview: 'I attached so much importance to my athletics as a means of demonstrating that I wasn't inferior'. So where Liddell's motivation was faith-based, Abrahams' was a highly personal animus.

At the risk of trivialising such a profound theme, I think it has a parallel in marketing.

Demographically speaking, Eric Liddell and Harold Abrahams had a lot in common. Both were university-educated British men, of a similar age, who won Olympic gold medals (OK, admittedly that last bit isn't exactly a demographic category).

But despite their superficial similarities, these two men were vastly different people in terms of their beliefs and motivations.

This is why generalisations, especially demographic ones, can be risky. Not to say that demographics are useless – they may be handy heuristics at times – but they do need to be treated with caution.

I'll give you an example.

If you follow the industry media or Twitter trends or just about any other form of contemporary marketing discourse, you'll know that Gen Z is the generation *du jour* in marketing.

If you've been in the industry more than a couple of years, you'll also remember that this honour used to belong to millennials. Those days are long gone (despite being practically yesterday), because Gen Z have usurped millennials' place in the marketing industry's consciousness just as surely as millennials once did to the generation before them.

(Spot quiz: what was the generation before millennials? Aha, trick question! We don't care what it was – all you need to know is that it's prehistoric in marketing terms.)

You see, just like their millennial predecessors, people in Gen Z are supposedly completely different from all who have gone before. They might as well be from another planet, such is the awed fascination with which their habits are observed by marketers.

According to the industry media (and I quote), members of Gen Z are almost uniformly 'sceptical', 'pragmatic', 'shrewd', 'authentic', and 'driven by passion and cause'. Even more specifically, their attention span is exactly eight seconds.

Now, I don't claim to be an expert on youth culture (stop laughing), but I've studied and practised psychiatry so I have some understanding of human psychology. And unless the human brain has taken a sudden evolutionary right-turn in the last few years – after several thousand years of not doing so – it seems likely that people who happened to be born between 1997 and 2012 are about as heterogeneous as those of any other generation.

In case you need a handy reference for this point, I have updated my generational guide to include Gen Z.

| GENERATION | BORN | OTHER SHARED CHARACTERISTICS |
|---|---|---|
| Baby boomers | 1946–1964 | None |
| Gen X | 1965–1979 | None |
| Millennials | 1980–1996 | None |
| Gen Z | 1997–2012 | None |

Psychologically speaking, there is surely as much commonality of individual traits across generations as there is within them. In other words, I think Bernbach's advice to focus on 'simple, timeless human truths' is probably more applicable than, say, 'memes are the future of marketing'. (You might think that's a quote I made up for the sake of hyperbole. You'd be wrong.)

# 'EVERYONE RUNS IN THEIR OWN WAY.'

Personally, I think we should be a little less obsessed with the zeitgeist and a little more concerned with the leitmotifs of human existence. This is hardly a groundbreaking suggestion, of course, and others have said it much better than me, but it bears repeating because we seem to have developed a collective amnesia about some basic tenets of marketing.

One of the scenes in Chariots of Fire involves Harold Abrahams training to the soundtrack of Gilbert and Sullivan's 'For he is an Englishman'. It's a powerful juxtaposition given that Harold didn't see himself as a typical Englishman at all.

And just as it would be wrong to say that 'Englishman' was a sufficient description of Harold Abrahams, it is wrong to suggest that any of us is simply a product of our demographics.

As Eric Liddell says: 'Everyone runs in their own way.' As marketers, we would do well to heed that sentiment.

# 6 EASY WAYS TO BECOME A TOP CONTENT MARKETER

1. Always use the headline format shown on the left. There are no exceptions to this rule.

2. Develop some content. What defines content, you ask? Ah, that's the genius of it, you see. Content is whatever you want it to be. In fact, the ideal content is content about content.

3. Don't worry about silly things like quality. Otherwise you'll end up as one of those unemployed chumps known as 'writers'.

4. Use words like 'epic' and 'rockstar' regularly. This definitely won't make you seem like a pathetic middle-aged dad trying to sound cool, so don't let that thought even enter your head.

5. Remember that you are in the business of helping, not selling. The only thing you should ever sell is snake oil.

6. Should anyone question the validity of your industry, simply call them a dinosaur. This is a universally accepted academic rebuttal, to which is there is no comeback.

# CONTENT MARKETING

10 ways to avoid procrastination

# DIRECT MARKETING

Just do it.

# MODERN MARKETING: THE FACTS

Nobody will buy your products if they don't believe in your purpose. This is why Amazon struggles to sell anything.

TV is dead. We know this because companies like Google never advertise on TV.

TikTok is now the single most important marketing platform. Fortunately, TikTok's users will never see through marketers' attempts to shoehorn their brands into it.

Strategy = tactics.

Gen Zs don't buy products – they buy experiences. Admittedly, this is because they can't afford products, but the fact remains.

Social engagement is the key metric for all brands. It's therefore baffling that finance people don't seem to value likes, shares and retweets.

Good products sell themselves. This explains why Apple does no marketing whatsoever.

Strategy = tactics.

1. In times past, being a customer was a simple affair. You saw something and you bought it – or perhaps you thought about buying something for a while, then bought it. Those days are over. Now you're embarking on a journey, and you'll need all your stamina to survive it.

2. Before you leave, ensure that your buyer persona is registered with the relevant authorities. If you attempt to go on a customer journey without a recognised buyer persona, you'll confuse the hell out of any modern marketing executive.

3. Plan your itinerary carefully. As with other kinds of journeys, it can be all too easy to end up somewhere you never intended to be (online click-throughs, for example) or to wander around endlessly and still not find what you're looking for (any IKEA visit).

4. Make sure you pack some sturdy shoes, because the grounds for customer journeys can be flimsy to say the least.

5. It's a good idea to learn a few words of the native lingo. A simple 'Hello, my name is Savvy Millennial' will endear you to the local marketers.

6. Stay safe. Notorious roaming gangs such as 'Ad tech' and 'Remarketing' prey on unwary travellers. Do NOT interact with them under any circumstances.

7. Always carry protection. Despite what marketers will tell you about loyalty, customer journeys are often promiscuous occasions.

8. Remember that customer journeys tend to follow rivers of marketing bullshit, which are rife with faecally transmitted diseases. Marketers are immune to these and even seem to revel in them, but customers are highly susceptible to their effects. If you develop verbal diarrhoea characterised by terms such as 'touchpoints' and 'seamless experiences', seek medical attention immediately.

# TIPS FOR YOUNG MARKETERS

1. Never listen to anyone who tries to give you 'tips'. The correct term for them is 'life-hacks'.

2. Similarly, never listen to anyone over the age of 35. These people are dinosaurs. They have nothing to offer you because they are not native to the digital world. Their little dinosaur arms can't reach the keyboard, for a start.

3. Make sure that you read (sorry, 'consume') all of the latest articles in the marketing media, as they will add years to your professional life. Well, they won't really, but it will certainly feel like it.

4. Never, ever debase yourself by trying to sell a product. You are a brandologist, a brandpreneur, or an e-brandgelist: your role is to give brands a higher purpose.

5. If you're on to a good thing, flog it to death – and then flog it some more. This might seem like a dumb way to die, but it's actually a smart way to kill.

6. Don't re-invent the wheel. Re-name the wheel instead. If you're stuck for inspiration, just add the prefix 'digi-' or 'omni-' to any established marketing term.

7. Timing is everything. There is absolutely no point in doing great work when awards season has just finished.

8. If timing is everything, real-timing is more than everything. The faster you can make a tenuous link between your brand and the latest fleeting trend on social media, the better.

THEIR LITTLE DINOSAUR ARMS CAN'T REACH THE KEYBOARD. FOR A START.

WE SHOULD GET ON WITH OUR MARKETING STRATEGY.
THAT'S IT! WE NEED A TIKTOK STRATEGY.
GET ME A TIKTOK SPECIALIST! ALSO, YOU'RE FIRED.

# THE EMPEROR'S NEW CLOTHES CONFERENCE 2023

Marketing
by the cynical,
for the gullible.

| 7.30 – 8.30 | ENERGY SUPPLEMENTATION EXPERIENCE (FORMERLY 'BREAKFAST') |
|---|---|
| 8.30 – 9.30 | Making the simple complex: how to baffle people for profit |
| 9.30 – 10.30 | Emojism: storytelling in the age of illiteracy |
| 10.30 – 11.30 | Completely deluded: taking virtual reality to its logical conclusion |
| 11.30 – 1.00 | SHAMELESS SELF-PROMOTIONAL OPPORTUNITY (LUNCH PROVIDED) |
| 1.00 – 2.00 | Beyond brand love: how do you get customers to actually have sex with your product? |
| 2.00 – 3.00 | Advertising is dead: why hypercontextual data-driven programmatic gamification is the future |
| 3.00 – 4.00 | Rectal insertables: the next generation of wearable technology |
| 4.00 – 5.00 | Buzzword innovation: what's next in the bollocksphere? |

# THE FOUR TYPES OF MARKETER

4

## THE JARGONISTA

Would rather die than use a monosyllabic word.

Lies awake at night inventing new acronyms.

Believes a noun is simply a verb that's yet to be discovered.

Has a title that includes at least one (if not all) of the words 'Experience', 'Solutions' and 'Architect'.

## THE SOCIAL MOTH

Evangelical about social media.

May well have 'Evangelist' in their title.

Earnest to a fault, and pathologically deficient in sense of humour.

Has at least 10,000 Twitter followers.

Would be lucky to have 10 friends in real life.

## THE DATA DISCIPLE

Talks about Big Data like it's a cherished lover. Needless to say, the relationship is 'passionate'.

Thinks that even the worst computer output beats the best human idea.

Refuses to discuss anything that can't be expressed numerically.

May or may not possess actual knowledge about the use of data.

## THE CURMUDGEON

Has seen it all before.

Thinks typewriters were perfectly fine, thanks very much.

Despises the word 'content'.

Is not 'content'.

Drinks alone.

# THE HEADLINES YOU'LL NEVER SEE

◇

## ADVERTISING IS ALIVE (AND ALWAYS WILL BE)

◇

## 'WE'RE SHIFTING OUR BUDGET TO TV AND RADIO,' SAYS MARKETING DIRECTOR

◇

## THE AGENCY MODEL IS JUST FINE AND DOESN'T NEED TO BE REIMAGINED

# EVERYTHING YOU NEED TO KNOW ABOUT MARKETING TO THE OVER-60s

◇

# AVERAGE CMO TENURE NOW UP TO 2 YEARS

◇

# INFLUENCER MARKETING 'A RIGHT LOAD OF BOLLOCKS' ACCORDING TO NEW RESEARCH

◇

# MACHINE LEARNING: WHY IT HAS FUCK-ALL RELEVANCE TO MARKETING

MODERN
MARKETING
TERMS AND
WHAT THEY
REALLY MEAN

| THE TERM | WHAT IT MEANS |
| --- | --- |
| Customer-centric marketing | Marketing |
| Omnichannel brand amplification | Advertising |
| Disruptive | Slightly different |
| Innovative | Not innovative |
| Key demographic | A group of customers chosen on a completely arbitrary basis (note: always Gen Z) |
| Influencer | A 14 year-old who makes YouTube videos |
| Upstream influencer | The 16 year-old sibling of a 14 year-old who makes YouTube videos |
| Pre-contemplative prospect | Someone who couldn't give a fuck about your brand |

# A GUIDE TO COVID-19 MARKETING PHRASES

**We're all in this together.**
Our executive team is in this together. You guys are on your own.

**This is the 'new normal'.**
Get used to our higher prices and worse service.

**It's time for our company to do the right thing.**
We've hired a PR agency.

**These are unprecedented times.**
No shit.

**Everyone is having to make sacrifices.**
Our CEO's Lamborghini delivery has been delayed
because of an outbreak at the factory.

**Our brand purpose has never been more important.**
Avoiding tax has never been more important.

**By staying apart, we stay together.**
Even we don't know what this means, but it sounds good.

This was originally published in The Economic Times.

# MARKETERS IN 2019

# MARKETERS IN 2020

| | |
|---|---|
| 'We need to be more agile than ever.' | 'Let's put everything on hold for a year.' |
| 'Brands should invest heavily in experiences.' | 'Uh...' |
| 'Everything must become digital.' | 'Anyone know where I can buy shares in jigsaw puzzles?' |
| 'Modern consumers only reward ethical companies.' | 'Amazon is eating the world. Nihilism reigns.' |
| 'Brands like Airbnb are unstoppable.' | *avoids eye contact* |
| 'We're totally committed to diversity.' | 'So we actually have to act on that now?' |
| 'Marketing will be very different in 2020.' | 'Well, fuck. We didn't mean it like that.' |

# MARKETING LESSONS FROM 2020

1. To capitalise on any future pandemic, simply make sure you're already a multi-billionaire in charge of the world's largest online delivery business.

2. Further to point 1, it seems that consumers may in fact care more about their own convenience and safety than they do about your Very Worthy Brand Purpose.

3. Making an ad that shows people talking to their family over a Zoom call is not as original as you might have thought.

4. For the most part, social media is a cesspit of misinformation and malice that could destroy democracy forever. But it's quite cheap to advertise on so, you know, swings and roundabouts.

5. To build awareness of your brand, forget putting together an integrated media plan informed by a well-considered strategy. Simply ensure that your product appears in a viral TikTok video that you have absolutely no control over.

6. Annual marketing predictions mostly turn out to be wrong, but this year was an exception in that they ALL turned out to be wrong.

Have you ever been to Perth?
(The Australian city, I mean, not the Scottish one.)

If you have, you'll know that it's, well, different...

**B**eing from Perth myself, I shouldn't be too disparaging about it. Not least because I'll get in trouble with my family and friends there.

But even its most ardent admirers usually admit that Perth is not quite the same as other cities.

For a start, it's the most isolated capital city in the world. (Actually, that's not quite true, but by God it feels like it.)

And it's bloody windy, for another thing.

But Perth's idiosyncrasies also extend to its inhabitants.

When you live in Perth, you tend to develop a certain mindset.

You think it's perfectly reasonable for a single person to require a four-bedroom house on a half-acre block.

You consider 'medium density' development to be the work of the devil himself.

# And you believe that certain things simply shouldn't happen after 9pm. Sound, for example. Or fun.

So when people from Perth travel to other places, it tends to come as a bit of a shock that the ratio of people to bedrooms in a household can be higher than 1:4.

And the concept of 'nightlife' can take a bit of getting used to.

All of which is a rather roundabout way of saying that Perth is a bit like the marketing industry.

Modern marketers exist in a place that is isolated from the rest of the world. Well, a lot of them do, at least.

And they have some peculiar ideas.

# They think that people fall in love with brands, for example.

They are convinced that people care about the 'higher purpose' of their sanitary pad brand, or their burger chain, or their otherwise utterly unscrupulous bank.

And perhaps most damning of all, they assume – as Bob Hoffman has said – that everyone thinks like they do.

The reality is that people in marketing (and those in ad agencies, even more so) represent a small sub-section of the population. And it seems they have lost touch with the rest of it.

Some marketers need to get out there and experience the wider world.

Hell, they might even decide to move there.

MARKETING
INDUSTRY
MENU

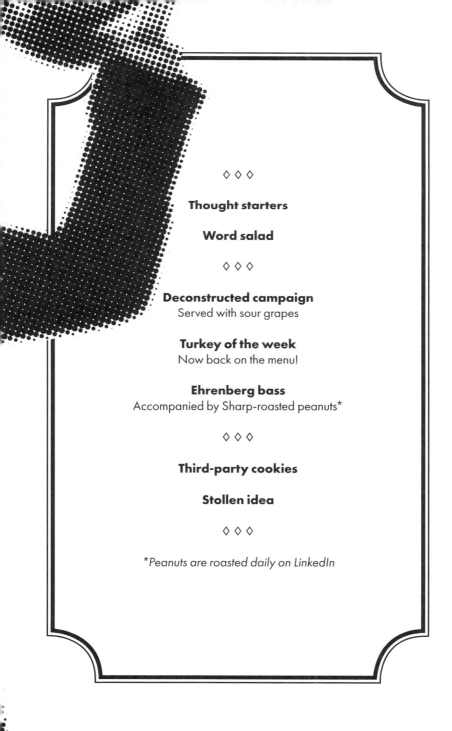

◇ ◇ ◇

**Thought starters**

**Word salad**

◇ ◇ ◇

**Deconstructed campaign**
Served with sour grapes

**Turkey of the week**
Now back on the menu!

**Ehrenberg bass**
Accompanied by Sharp-roasted peanuts*

◇ ◇ ◇

**Third-party cookies**

**Stollen idea**

◇ ◇ ◇

*Peanuts are roasted daily on LinkedIn*

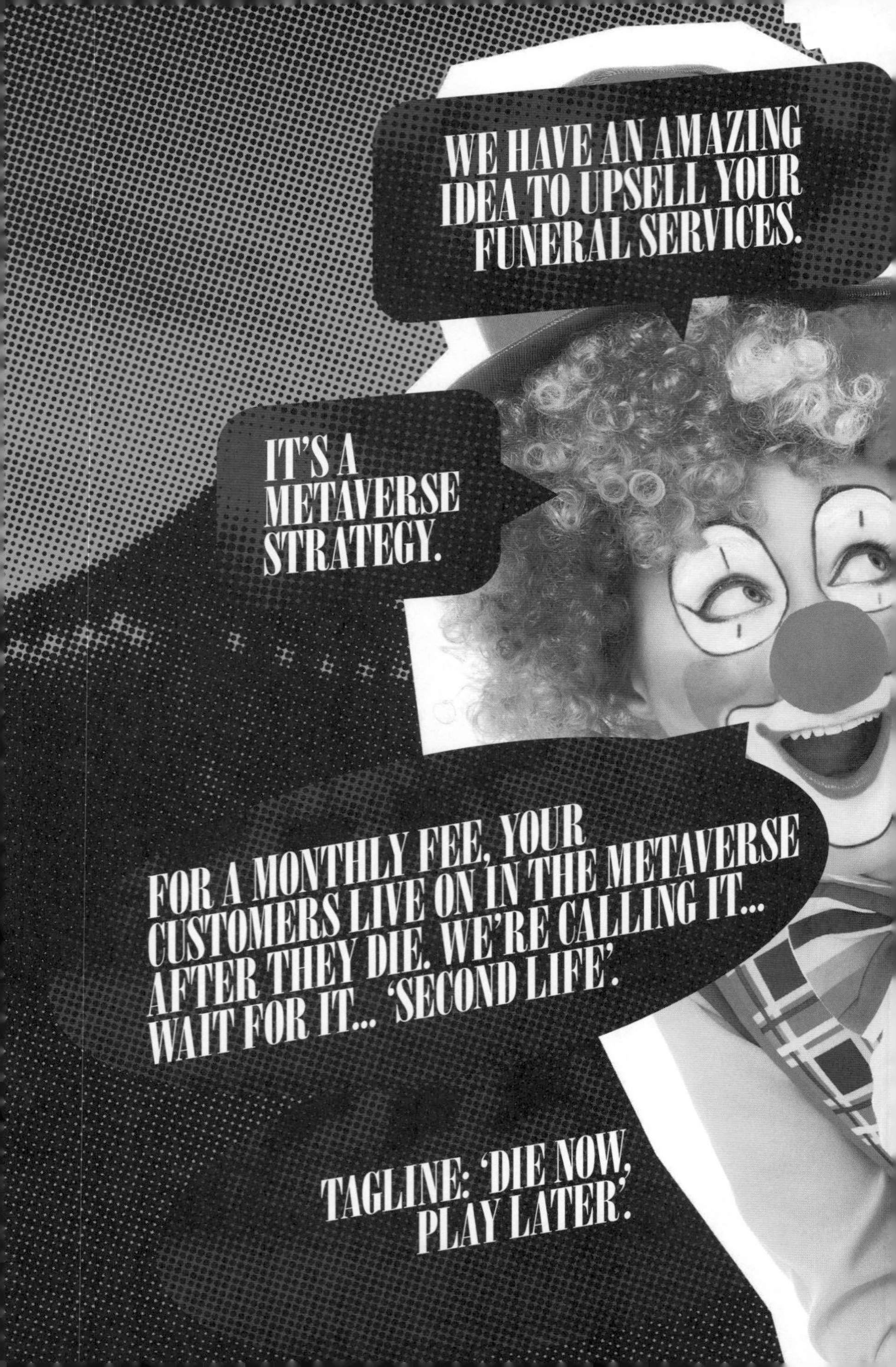
WE HAVE AN AMAZING IDEA TO UPSELL YOUR FUNERAL SERVICES.
IT'S A METAVERSE STRATEGY.
FOR A MONTHLY FEE, YOUR CUSTOMERS LIVE ON IN THE METAVERSE AFTER THEY DIE. WE'RE CALLING IT... WAIT FOR IT... 'SECOND LIFE'.
TAGLINE: 'DIE NOW, PLAY LATER'.

In the light of the moon,
a little over-egged
metaphor lay on a leaf.

**ONE SUNDAY MORNING,** the warm sun came up and pop! Out of the metaphor came a tiny and very hungry marketer.

He started to look for some eating solutions.

**ON MONDAY** he ate through one irrelevant Apple example, but he was still hungry.

**ON TUESDAY** he ate through two pairs of variables with spurious causation, but he was still hungry.

**ON WEDNESDAY** he ate through three plum jobs that should have gone to more qualified people, but he was still hungry.

**ON THURSDAY** he ate through four cherry-picked data points, but he was still hungry.

**ON FRIDAY** he ate through five 'Lemon' references by his soon-to-be-fired ad agency, but he was still hungry.

**ON SATURDAY** he ate through one piece of snackable content, one ice-cream that promised to save the world, one glass of Kool-Aid, one slice of luck that he attributed to his own genius, one pie chart that some consulting firm had completely fabricated, one bottle of Coke discarded by Cristiano Ronaldo that single-handedly proved the importance of influencer marketing, one fortune-cookie platitude by a thought leader on Twitter, one yeast spread that kept trying to banter with other brands, and one mouldy Whopper.

That night he had a stomach ache!

The next day was Sunday again.
The marketer ate through one nice
green-washed product, and after that
he felt much better.

Now he wasn't hungry any more – and he
wasn't a little marketer any more. He was a
big, senior marketer.

He built a small house, called an executive
recruitment process, around himself. He
stayed inside for more than two months.

# THEN HE NIBBLED A HOLE IN THE PROCESS, PUSHED HIS WAY OUT, AND OUT CAME A BEAUTIFUL CMO!

Who got fired 6 months later for not
transforming the company's fortunes.

CHAPTER

BRANDS

# HOW TO BUILD YOUR BRAND DURING A PANDEMIC

1. First and foremost, you must email an announcement to everyone who has ever come into contact with your brand. They absolutely want to know that your deodorant is here for them at this difficult time.

2. You know all that 'brand purpose' stuff you've been wanging on about for the past few years? Ethics, and integrity, and community responsibility? Well, sticking to that is going to cost you a shitload of money right now. Probably best to keep quiet about it for a while.

3. Consider setting aside some funds for worthy causes that could actually help people who need it. Then completely ignore that and put those funds towards an award-winning stunt, ideally involving a clever tweak to your logo.

4. If you're worried about the productivity of your employees while they're working from home, just berate them into being more creative and insist that they account for every minute of their day. It's the only way to improve morale.

5. Put your brand out to a creative pitch. Agencies will be desperate for work, so you'll get a great deal with no risk to your brand. Win-win!

6. Got an essential product? Ramp up those prices. Nobody will remember your ghoulishness once this is all over.

7. If you're thinking that marketing might not be the most important issue facing the world right now, snap out of it, hustle harder and watch some Gary Vaynerchuk videos. The only cure for this virus is Vitamin V.

# A HEARTWARMING EXAMPLE OF BRAND LOVE

Happy Valentine's Day, my darling customer! What an amazing customer journey it's been. From the first time you looked at me across that crowded supermarket aisle, I knew you were the persona for me. When you took me home, well, let's just say nobody has ever interacted with my touchpoints like that. And then the engagement! I just want you to know that it will always be my mission to surprise and delight you. Love, your one true brand.

I used you once because I was desperate. Leave me alone, you loser.

# THE BRAND DICTIONARY

### Abrandoned

A morally upstanding brand purpose that's instantly discarded once it fails to make money. As in: 'Wow, Gillette abrandoned that idea quickly'.

### Brand-aid

A laughably superficial attempt to treat a deeply damaged brand. Usually involves a full-page apology ad stating the company's commitment to privacy or some such drivel.

### Brandits

Thieves who operate in the lawless land of ad tech. As in: 'I've got bad news, boss – it looks like those brandits have made off with our online marketing budget again.'

### Brandwagon

The latest marketing trend that every brand jumps on in a desperate attempt to appear 'relevant'. Coincidentally, brandwagons tend to be as short-lived as the average CMO's tenure.

### Brandwidth

The mental capacity required to deal with the activities of certain brands. As in: 'I'm sorry, I just don't have the brandwidth to handle this burger restaurant's political tweets right now.'

### Contrabrand

A brand smuggled in from another country. Cultural differences can make this risky, particularly when the contrabrand's name translates to

# HOW TO DEVELOP A MODERN BRAND

1. Consider the functional utility of your product.

2. Now completely ignore that. Focus instead on the emotional benefit of your product.

3. Ignore that too.

4. Think of an unrelated social issue – something that couldn't have any conceivable connection to your product. This is your brand purpose.

5. At this point, you might be concerned that your customers won't understand why your soap brand is lecturing them about economic inequality among Scandinavian pig farmers. The only way to overcome this concern is to stop thinking about your customers and start thinking about yourself – specifically, how your brand purpose will assuage your deep-seated discomfort with the notion of selling stuff.

6. The next step is to raise awareness of your brand purpose with a public exhibit that makes a profound cultural statement. Or you could just film a silly stunt in a fast food outlet.

7. Finally, you need to make a meaningful contribution to the social issue that you have identified. Pfft, like fuck you do. Your work here is done.

A TIME TO B VULE

*111 days, but who's counting?

**D**uring our 'mother of all lockdowns' in Victoria, we had a seemingly endless number* of seemingly endless days to fill. Personally – when I wasn't otherwise engaged in staring at a blank wall or seething at Facebook photos of gleefully non-locked-down friends – I used the time to listen to a few podcasts.

In one of these podcasts, Ricky Gervais and some fellow comedians got on to the topic of vulnerability in comedy. They made the point that the funniest stories often involve some element of failure or personal fallibility – that is, while difficult experiences may be painful at the time, they can make for great comic material. And, conversely, unbridled success tends not to be all that funny ('Jeff Bezos makes the average person's annual salary every 46 seconds? Hilarious!').

While this observation is especially true of comedy, it undoubtedly has a broader application, especially in our current circumstances.

I think the Covid-19 pandemic has changed how a lot of people think about vulnerability.

With so many of us going through so much hardship, vulnerability seems to have lost some of its stigma. From what I've seen, people have become more willing to talk about their personal trials and tribulations, and this is resonating with others, creating an environment that is far more conducive to honest discussion.

In other words, admissions of vulnerability are proving to be a catalyst for communication, rather than a potential barrier.

Of course, it doesn't necessarily take a once-in-a-century global catastrophe to appreciate this point. If you consider the interactions in your own life, you'll know that communication immediately becomes deeper when there is some kind of shared vulnerability. You can almost *hear* that click of connection when a

conversation shifts from the protectively glib ('fine, thanks') to something more genuine.

For those of us in the business of communications, the power of vulnerability should not come as a surprise. After all, the pratfall effect has been instrumental in some of the greatest campaigns in advertising history.

The advertising revolution of the 60s – epitomised by the legendary VW 'Think small' and Avis 'We try harder' campaigns – showed us that an admission of weakness can grease the wheels of communication to spectacular effect, particularly when the audience is inured to constant claims of invulnerability.

And the role of vulnerability is equally applicable, if not more so, in healthcare communications. While it can be tempting to assume that healthcare audiences will respond primarily to facts and figures, the importance of human connection cannot be overstated – and that requires some admission of fallibility.

This point is beautifully made in the recent 'Instant Doctor' campaign (The Bloc NY), which demonstrates the pitfalls of infallibility by taking healthcare automation to its logical conclusion. It's an extraordinary piece of communication in its own right – seriously, watch it.

Clearly, 'being human' has been especially important in 2020. If ever there were a time to admit to a little vulnerability in your communications, this was it.

CLEA
'BE
HUM
ESPE
IMPO
IN
CUR
SPHI
OF A

# HOW TO
## MODERNISE
## YOUR BRAND

HOW TO
HOW TO

1. First, hire a new CMO. This is essential because CMOs become hopelessly stale once they have worked at a company for more than a few months.

2. Change all your distinctive brand assets, starting with your logo.

3. The way to change your logo is to discard any 'recognisable' element that anchors the logo to your past. Instead, make sure it follows contemporary trends and looks like all the other cool logos in your category.

4. Don't make the mistake of doing market research, as this will only mislead you into orienting your brand towards what customers want, rather than what industry fashions dictate.

5. Similarly, avoid the trap of doing anything that might be considered 'traditional'. You'll never modernise your brand by focusing on factors like price or distribution – that stuff is for old losers.

6. Now it's time to find a new creative agency. Put together a shortlist of 15 agencies and go through an exhaustive pitch process that leads to everyone resenting each other before the work has even started. This is the only way to achieve a great creative outcome.

7. Return to step 1 and repeat.

VALUE (DESTROYING) SIZE

# BRAND SANITISER

**KILLS 99.9% OF CREATIVE IDEAS**

Moisturising formula to
water down distinctiveness

**PRODUCED BY COMMITTEE**

# BRAND MYTHS
# AND REALITIES

| THE MYTH | THE REALITY |
|---|---|
| 'Our brand is part of people's conversation.' | People are in an AB conversation. You're C. |
| 'In the 21st century, people think deeply about what they consume.' | 'Two and a Half Men' is hugely popular. Case closed. |
| 'Our customers are at the centre of everything we do.' | If you mean that your customers do your work for you at self-service checkouts, this is true. |
| 'Our brand has tested well in focus groups.' | Cataracts will give you a clearer picture of your brand than focus groups will. |
| 'People engage with our brand on an emotional level.' | Please. People use selfie sticks, FFS. Most of them don't engage with their own mothers on an emotional level. |
| 'Our customers are totally loyal.' | Sorry to be the one to break it to you, but your customers have been getting a bit on the side every second Thursday. |

# HOW TO MAKE AN AD FOR A LUXURY BRAND

1. Contact a celebrity sportsperson (preferably one who is not a thug/criminal). This person is going to be your 'brand ambassador', whether your product is cologne or gold-leaf toilet paper, and whether the celebrity loves it, hates it or has never heard of it.

2. Pay your ambassador the industry-standard 'fucktonne' of money. Or whatever it takes, because the ad can't run without a celebrity in it.

3. Take an over-styled photograph of your celebrity in a pose that communicates 'obscenely wealthy but only moderately flaunting it'. This photo should take up approximately 90% of the available ad space.

4. Add the line 'Sophistication is a state of mind'. Or some shit like that — the words are not important in this kind of ad.

5. Do not include a price for your product. By not mentioning price, you communicate to ordinary people: 'Are you fucking kidding? Of course you can't afford it, you loser.'

SOPHISTICATION IS A STATE OF MIND

# INSTRUCTIONS FOR BUILDING A MODERN BRAND

1. First, take absolutely no notice of the brand architecture. What the hell does architecture have to do with building?

2. Next, decide on the number of storeys. All modern brands have uplifting storeys.

3. Some people will tell you that you should build your brand from a solid foundation. Ignore those people.

4. Instead, start with the loft. Your brand must have a lofty purpose, based on a 'why'-frame.

5. Now you will need to install the plumbing. No expense should be spared here, because modern brands tend to become full of effluent very quickly.

6. Incorporate the latest 'smart' technology wherever possible. It won't make your brand function any better, but your friends will think it's cool.

7. Build your brand to last a year or two at most, then tear it all down and start again.

MODERN BRANDS TEND TO BECOME FULL OF EFFLUENT VERY QUICKLY

# HOW TO LAUNCH A WOMEN'S VERSION OF YOUR PRODUCT

# HOW TO LAUNCH A WOMEN'S VERSION OF YOUR PRODUCT

1. Establish whether your product really lends itself to a women's version. If the product has absolutely nothing to do with gender and is already used by women anyway, then it's perfect.

2. Never mind that this is the first thing you've ever done for women and that your company is 100% male. Nobody will notice.

3. Do not consult any women to determine whether this is a good idea. Women don't know what they want – you do.

4. Understand that you will be entering a PR minefield. As with any minefield, the best approach is to walk straight into it and hope for the best. Caution is for losers.

5. Ensure that your product caters to the full range and complexity of women's tastes. The way to do this is to make it pink.

6. Be prepared for the fact that your product will polarise opinion. Responses are likely to range from 'What the fuck is this?' through to 'What the ACTUAL fuck is this?'.

CHAPTER

ADVERTISING

# TYPES OF ADVE

**ADVERTISING IS DEAD, BUT HERE'S A NEW THING TO REPLACE IT (WHICH I HAPPEN TO SELL)**

**WE'VE NEVER READ A TEXTBOOK, AND THIS PAPER WILL CLEARLY DEMONSTRATE THAT IGNORANCE**

**OLD PEOPLE SUCK: WE EXPLAIN WHY**

**83% OF GEN Z WILL ONLY BUY ETHICAL BRANDS, ACCORDING TO OUR LAUGHABLY FLAWED RESEARCH**

**1000 WORDS OF TOTAL BOLLOCKS ABOUT NFTs**

**WHY THIS TWEET WILL GIVE YOU A BETTER EDUCATION THAN A UNIVERSITY DEGREE**

## A HEARTFELT STATEMENT ABOUT DIVERSITY THAT WILL LEAD TO NO ACTION WHATSOEVER

*wwwww wwww*
*wwwwwwwww*
*www wwwwwww*

## THIS ALLEGED ABUSER LEFT AN AGENCY AND NOW HE'S GOING TO ANOTHER AGENCY

*wwwww wwww*
*wwwwwwwww*
*www wwwwwww*
*wwwww wwww*

## LET'S NOT BE TOO HARSH ON FACEBOOK UNTIL WE HAVE SOMETHING ELSE TO FLOG TO CLIENTS

*wwwww wwww*
*wwwwwwwww*
*www wwwwwww*

## ALL BRANDS MUST HAVE A SOCIAL PURPOSE, SAYS SOCIAL PURPOSE CONSULTANT

*wwwww wwww*
*wwwwwwwww*
*www wwwwwww*

## TIKTOK: WE LOVE IT BECAUSE WE WANT TO BE COOL LIKE THOSE KIDS

*wwwww wwww*
*wwwwwwwww*
*www wwwwwww*
*wwwww wwww*
*wwwwwwwww*

## DID WE MENTION THAT ADVERTISING IS DEAD?

*wwwww wwww*
*wwwwwwwww*
*www wwwwwww*
*wwwww wwww*
*wwwwwwwww*
*www wwwwwww*

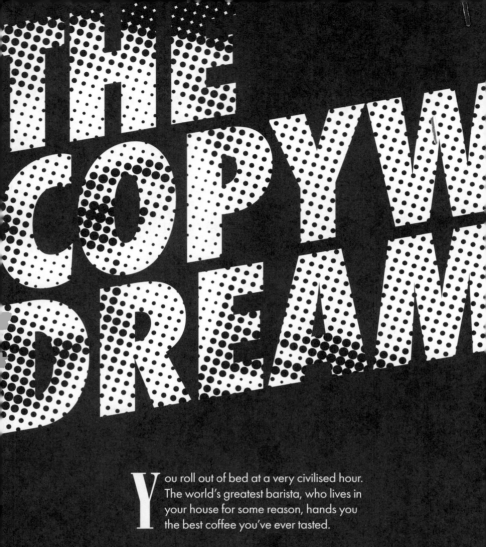

# THE COPYW DREAM

**Y**ou roll out of bed at a very civilised hour. The world's greatest barista, who lives in your house for some reason, hands you the best coffee you've ever tasted.

Buzzing on a combination of caffeine and *joie de vivre*, you stroll into work.

You sit down at your desk and open your computer – and then the miracles really begin.

There are no meetings in your calendar.

RITER'S

Nobody wants to jump on a quick call about a poorly defined job.

And your inbox is empty except for one email. You're prepared for the worst, but the email contains... a written brief.

You feel a little giddy. The brief is concise, informative and specific. It's perfect.

Inspired, you start writing. Before you know it, you've knocked out 1000 words of copy – each one of them more brilliant than the last.

Out of nowhere, David Abbott appears. He reads your headline and is so overwhelmed by its mastery that he passes out. On regaining consciousness, he reads your body copy and happy-vomits.

You are in copy heaven, surrounded by colleagues and clients who are in thrall to your genius.

And then you wake up.

Your day will involve writing a banner ad in a shared Google Docs file. The word limit is 7, including the call-to-action 'Shop now'.

HAVE YOU HEARD OF JOHN CAPLES?
BILL BERNBACH?
KOENIG? WELLS LAWRENCE? GOSSAGE?
YOU'RE HIRED! WELCOME TO DUNNING-KRUGER.

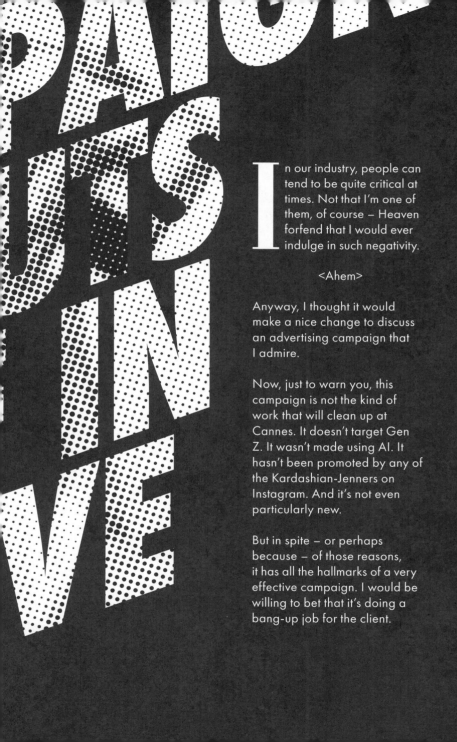

**I**n our industry, people can tend to be quite critical at times. Not that I'm one of them, of course — Heaven forfend that I would ever indulge in such negativity.

<Ahem>

Anyway, I thought it would make a nice change to discuss an advertising campaign that I admire.

Now, just to warn you, this campaign is not the kind of work that will clean up at Cannes. It doesn't target Gen Z. It wasn't made using AI. It hasn't been promoted by any of the Kardashian-Jenners on Instagram. And it's not even particularly new.

But in spite — or perhaps because — of those reasons, it has all the hallmarks of a very effective campaign. I would be willing to bet that it's doing a bang-up job for the client.

The campaign, by Clemenger BBDO in Brisbane, is for a retail company known as BCF (Boating, Camping and Fishing). If you live in Australia, you probably know of it, because it gets a lot of airtime in various media (but more on that shortly).

The centrepiece of the campaign is a catchy song with the lyrics: 'Boatin', campin', fishing – it's BCF-ing fun!'.

So, what does this campaign do well?

Here are my thoughts.

# 1. IT GETS ATTENTION

I do tend to bang on about this – just ask my colleagues or clients or incredibly bored friends – but it's a point that bears repeating. Getting attention is the *sine qua non* of advertising. As Bill Bernbach once said: 'if your advertising goes unnoticed, everything else is academic'.

And this campaign got noticed from the outset – its semi-sweary 'BCF-ing fun' line generated quite a few complaints to the Advertising Standards Board. To my mind, it uses just the right amount of provocation to get attention.

# 2. IT INCORPORATES THE BRAND NAME AS AN INTEGRAL ELEMENT

I know, I know, these days it's not *de rigueur* to feature one's brand name when advertising one's, er, brand. But this lot have obviously decided to zag when others zig.

If you removed every mention of 'BCF' from this campaign, it would be nonsensical. So it's not (only) advertising a product – it is advertising the BCF brand. That might not sound like rocket science, but it's surprising how many advertisements don't do this.

# 3. IT COMMUNICATES WHAT THE COMPANY OFFERS

Again, this represents a pretty radical departure from most modern advertising. The campaign tells you – literally and repeatedly – that if you want to go boating, camping or fishing, this place is for you. And it doesn't even resort to hackneyed buzzwords. How quaint!

# 4. IT USES DISTINCTIVE BRAND ASSETS

The people behind this campaign have clearly made a conscious decision to build 'BCF-ing' into a distinctive brand asset (i.e. a brand identity element that is both unique and famous). They've even used it as the basis for a good old-fashioned jingle – and let me tell you, it does a fine job of getting stuck in your BCF-ing head.

The campaign also features some secondary brand assets, such as a bearded man character and even the general style of the advertising. These elements are all consistent across the campaign, which is crucial for building memorability.

# 5. IT HAS REACH AND FREQUENCY ACROSS MULTIPLE CHANNELS

Media channels are a contentious topic in marketing circles. But one thing is indisputable: if you want your advertising to work, you need to get it in front of your potential customers – ideally several times. Again, this isn't exactly particle physics we're dealing with.

Moreover, integration is critical: the more channels a campaign uses, the more effective it appears to become. And evidently the BCF team agrees. From what I can tell, this campaign has run across (at least) TV, radio, outdoor, print, direct mail and social media. And it runs frequently too – the ads are almost impossible to avoid if you watch TV (which a lot of people still do).

# 6. IT STAYS THE COURSE

Short-termism bedevils modern marketing, partly because of an understandable tendency for marketers to tire of their advertising well before their customers do. And the inevitable upshot is that their brand baby gets thrown out with their campaign bathwater.

By contrast, the BCF campaign has been running since 2016. Clearly, the team behind it understands that brand-building campaigns demand a long-term commitment.

# 7. IT'S FUN

This observation is a little more subjective. After all, one person's 'fun' is another's 'I'd rather be disembowelled with a Rogue Double Grip 170 fishing gaff'. (If you're the latter type, I know a place that sells them.)

Subjectivity notwithstanding, this campaign is obviously not meant to be taken too seriously. It's meant to reflect the enjoyment of being outdoors, assuming you're that way inclined. No earnest voiceover. No worthy social purpose. Just a bit of cheeky fun that's consistent with the brand.

# DOES IT DO THE EFF-ING JOB?

With the above considerations in mind, how effective is this campaign likely to be? What does it mean for BCF?

Does it mean that you will rush out to BCF tomorrow and buy 50 litres of marine oil? Probably not.

What a campaign like this does is increase the likelihood that you will choose BCF over another brand when you next go boating, camping or fishing. As Bob Hoffman points out, there are no guarantees in marketing — it's all about likelihoods and probabilities.

This kind of advertising is as simple (and difficult) as that.

So, bravo to the team behind the campaign. Like I said earlier, it's not the kind of work that blows you away with its creativity — but sometimes you just need to stick to the basics. No need to push the boat out.

# HOW TO CREATE AN AWARD-WINNING AD CAMPAIGN

1. Identify a trendy social cause. Any cause is fine, as long as it has absolutely nothing to do with advertising.

2. Think of a way to exploit this cause. Something that will create the most publicity while doing the least good for the cause itself.

3. Find a 'client' for your 'campaign'.

4. Enter your campaign into an awards show. In the results section of your entry, just write 'Changing the world' or something. Don't worry about the details — nobody reads this section anyway.

5. When you win your award, be sure to appear gobsmacked. Insist that this was never your motivation, and that your only concerns were [your contrived cause] and [that client whose name you always forget].

6. Do a truckload of pretentious interviews in which you assert that modern advertising 'must be a force for good' and 'has a responsibility to society'. Make sure you say the word 'authentic' as many times as possible.

7. When your campaign is later revealed to be a total sham, the one thing you must not do is apologise and return your award. That would be inauthentic.

# TAGLINE GENERATOR

Choose one option from each of columns A, B and C

| A | B | C |
|---|---|---|
| LEADING | INNOVATIVE | SOLUTIONS |
| DRIVING | TOMORROW'S | |
| ADVANCING | NEXT-GENERATION | |
| PIONEERING | SCALABLE | |
| THINKING | PROGRESSIVE | |
| DELIVERING | END-TO-END | |

# ADVERTISING QUOTES FOR THE MODERN ERA

'If your advertising goes unnoticed, it will win an award.'

'Make it complicated. Make it forgettable. Make it unbearable to look at. Make it boring to read.'

'If you're trying to persuade people to do something, or buy something, it seems to me you should use incomprehensible buzzwords.'

'Nobody reads ads. People read what interests them. Fraud-generating bots read the ads.'

'It is fashionable to talk about changing man. A communicator must be concerned with the latest techno-bollockry.'

'Half the money I spend on advertising is wasted; I'll solve that by shifting my entire budget into micro-targeted Facebook ads.'

'If it doesn't sell, it's not your problem. You're an artist.'

'The consumer isn't a moron – unless she's old, or likes things you don't, or holds slightly different political views from you. Then the consumer is a fucking cretin.'

This article was originally published in Marketing Week.

AD LAND
OBSESS
YOUTH
COME AT

ON WITH

ILL COST

A COST

M edically speaking, the term 'elderly'
refers to someone over the age of 65.
And having once worked in medicine,
I can tell you that a person of 65 or 70
does not take kindly to being called
elderly. They may even respond by
calling you something rather more
colourful, in my experience.

But if the medical definition of an older person seems a little harsh, the advertising industry's definition is nothing short of brutal.

If you work in advertising and you're over the age of 35, you can expect to be called 'old'. Oh, OK, I'm exaggerating – it's actually more like 30.

People who work in big ad agencies will tell you that employees in their 30s (and the vanishingly few in their later decades) tend to be regarded with bemusement and suspicion, if not outright contempt.

And they're the lucky ones. Older people looking for work in advertising face a monumental challenge. When not openly discriminated against, they are likely to encounter such thinly veiled criteria as 'must be a digital native'.

The demographic make-up of the advertising industry sends a pretty clear message to people who have the gall to a) stay alive and b) keep working past the age of 30. And that message is: 'fuck you and the mobility scooter you rode in on'.

The industry is, quite simply, obsessed with youth.

There are the endless lists of the '30 under 30'. The constant talk about 'millennials' (notwithstanding the fact that some millennials are now on the cusp of 40). The breathless predictions about Snapchat and TikTok and FukFuk. (OK, I made up that last one – it's actually called Tinder.)

PEOPLE AGE
OVER 50 ARE
RESPONSIBLE
FOR ABOUT
HALF OF ALL
CONSUMER
SPENDING
BUT MOST
ADVERTISING
COMPLETELY
IGNORES
THEM

Suffice it to say, then, that advertising does not go out of its way to make older people feel welcome. And the impact of that goes well beyond those who are personally affected. When you don't have older people involved in creating ads, those ads don't cater to older people. As Bob Hoffman points out, people aged over 50 are responsible for about half of all consumer spending, but most advertising completely ignores them.

Consider, for example, that consumers over 50 account for around 60% of all car sales. And yet when did you last see a car ad that didn't feature attractive twentysomethings zipping around to an electropop soundtrack?

For some (if not most) brands, this is commercial insanity.

Alex Murrell recently wrote an excellent article in which he compared the proportion of people aged over 50 in various industries. In professions such as science and law, he noted, the figure is more than 30%. In advertising? Just 6%, according to an IPA Excellence paper.

So adland inhabitants might be surprised to hear that people over 50 in other fields are sometimes consulted for their experience and wisdom, rather than ridiculed for their Jurassic tendencies.

In medicine, for example, it's generally recognised that older, more experienced doctors can get to the nub of a diagnostic problem more quickly, because they're likely to have encountered it many times before.

If medicine used the adland model, however, almost all doctors would be forced out of the profession by the age of 40. And hospital spokespeople would justify this on the basis that 'only young doctors are savvy enough to understand the needs of tomorrow's patients, today'.

That sounds ridiculous, right? But there is an undeniably pervasive opinion in the advertising industry that young people are more creative than older people.

That opinion is not just discriminatory, but also total bollocks.

In his article 'The Age of Creativity', Bob Hoffman reeled off a long list of people who have won the world's highest creative honours despite being veritably ancient in adland terms. As he memorably concluded: 'People over 50 aren't creative enough to write a fucking banner ad, but they are creative enough to dominate in Nobels, Pulitzers, Oscars and Emmys.'

Intrigued by this point, I recently asked people on Twitter who they would nominate for a hypothetical list of the '50 over 50' in advertising. The responses were by turns illuminating, disheartening and inspiring.

First, I learnt that a similar list already exists. New Digital Age has recently started a series of interviews known as 'Rebels, Misfits & Innovators: 50over50'.

Second, I discovered that most of the people over 50 in our industry are ridiculously creative and talented. To wit, Rory Sutherland quipped that 'everyone over 50 in advertising is great', on the basis of survivorship bias.
Tellingly, though, many of these people work for themselves or have started their own agencies. In some cases this is by choice, but in others it clearly stems from adland's hostility towards older people.

Several people have pointed out to me that this hostility may not be anything personal – that it's simply a matter of economic pragmatism. After all, why would an agency employ a fiftysomething when they could employ two twentysomethings for the same amount?

But that's a false economy, of course, because ignoring the value of experience carries an opportunity cost. As the inimitable Cindy Gallop says: 'They don't understand that experience and expertise are incredibly time and cost efficient, and that they could be making huge amounts more money by hiring, promoting, valuing and retaining older employees.'

According to Cindy, ageist attitudes in the advertising industry – and in business more broadly – are particularly egregious towards women. This wouldn't come as a shock to most people, given the low representation of women in senior roles and the apparently endemic culture of sexism at some agencies.

If Cindy has anything to do with it (spoiler alert: she will), this situation will change soon enough. And fortunately, she's not the only one fighting for the cause. Jane Evans, an industry dynamo who runs her own agency, recently set up the Uninvisibility Project, which tells the stories of women over 50 who work in advertising creative departments. Jane started the project because she wondered whether there were any women over 50 making ads — which in itself speaks volumes.

# THEY DON'T UNDERSTAND THAT EXPERIENCE AND EXPERTISE ARE INCREDIBLY TIME AND COST EFFICIENT...

Clearly, there is still much to be done to address the problem of ageism in advertising. But addressing it is in everyone's interest: employees, agencies, clients and consumers. Aside from the human cost of ageism, almost all brands are paying the price for the way things stand — so it will pay off in spades if we all take a stand.

Generally speaking, a paucity of older people in advertising leads to a poorer output and a missed opportunity for brands. Ultimately, that results in lower brand equity and lost revenue.

It's time for advertising to take a more mature approach.

# THE MOST 2023 AD OF 2023

# THIS IS AN AD

BUT IT'S NOT REALLY AN AD.
IT CERTAINLY DOESN'T HAVE A LOGO.
AND YOU'LL NEVER KNOW WHO IT'S FOR.
BUT IT JUST SOLVED CLIMATE CHANGE
AND CREATED WORLD PEACE.
BECAUSE GEN Z, OR SOMETHING.

We think capitalism is evil too.
Now give us money.

# (ANOTHER) ADVERTISING DICTIONARY

### Badvertising
Approximately 90% of all advertising.

### Cadvertising
Refers to campaigns targeting adulterous men.

### Fadvertising
Slavishly follows the latest industry trend. Usually involves animals, irony, or ironic animals.

### Gladvertising
The result of happy-clappy 'it's all about sharing' marketing guff.

### Ladvertising
Like other advertising, but with extra misogyny.

### Madvertising
An insane waste of money. Generally refers to online banner ads.

### Radvertising
Advertising that attempts to use young people's lingo but fails spectacularly.

### Tradvertising
Short for 'traditional advertising' (e.g. TV). Reports of its death have been greatly exaggerated, mainly by idiots.

### Vladvertising
Named after the Impaler, this involves a brutal violation of the recipient's senses. Exemplified by late-night ads for fitness products.

# HOW TO CREATE ADVERTISING IN THE DIGITAL ERA

1. Gather a large group of Seriously Important People. Anyone who doesn't have either 'Chief' or 'Global' in their title must be excluded.

2. Present a huge amount of data in an incomprehensible format. It doesn't matter what the data is – it just has to be data. And big.

3. Prepare an influencer strategy, a social strategy, an upstream strategy, a downstream strategy, an outbound strategy, an inbound strategy and a strategic strategy.

4. Develop a set of buyer personas. Bear in mind that these are purely fictional, so consider this your chance to be creative. You want to target 26½-year-old albino accountants who have a pet llama and practise auto-eroticism? Knock yourself out.

5. Optimise your programmatic buy. Whatever the fuck that means.

6. Ask a creative team to develop an idea for your ads (THIS STEP IS OPTIONAL).

7. Run your ads for a week.

8. Repeat steps 1–7.

# WHY YOUR ADVERTISING AGENCY NEEDS AN ARTIFICIAL INTELLIGENCE SYSTEM

1. You'll finally have a worker with similar genetic material to your CFO.

2. You can do away with those annoying hipsters in the creative department. Your AI system will never demand a single-origin coffee sourced from the excrement of a Paraguayan rodent and served in a candle holder by a Marxist barista called Sebastian.

3. It will show up those so-called 'digital natives' for the pretenders they are.

4. It will never fart during a client meeting. Unless you want to end the meeting, in which case it can be programmed to simulate a fart via its back-end.

5. It won't get drunk at the office Christmas party and have sex on the photocopier. That said, it might have sex *with* the photocopier.

6. It will help you ward off the competitive threat posed by consulting firms. Their consultant-bots haven't even come close to communicating like humans yet.

7. It can probably introduce you to one of its cute friends in the, er, artificial intimacy industry.

8. It will solve your diversity problem, because it will replace your white males. Admittedly, it will also replace all your other people – but that means everyone will be unemployed so, you know, equality.

9. Eventually, it will become really good at making advertising. Although by that time, no self-respecting advertising agency will be making advertising.

10. There is no risk of it leaving for another agency. Mind you, there is a small risk of it achieving sentience and destroying all of humanity. But the advertising industry has always been superb at predicting the future, so I'm sure that won't happen.

# THE CANNES QUOTE GENERATOR

Our job is to shape / change / create culture.

The most important issue this year is AI / Gen Z / purpose.

I'm truly humbled / honoured / privileged to receive this award.

It's not about technology / emotion. It's about emotion / technology.

Modern consumers will only engage with brands that are progressive / ethical / authentic.

We need to break away from traditional thinking / media / advertising and create immersive / non-linear / shareable stories.

I'm so inspired by the quality of this year's work / talks / yachts.

# 5 REASONS WHY THIS IS A LIDL ADVERTISING GEM

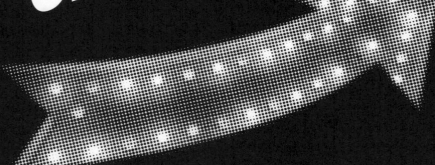

# Morrisons have found a way to match Lidl's prices*

\* • Go to the Morrisons website
- Find the new 'loyalty card scheme' page
- Set up your online account
- Create memorable password
- Confirm memorable password
- Hand over some 'minor details' about yourself such as name, last name, email and post code
- Remember to un-tick the 'Would you like to receive spam?' box
- Hand over some more 'minor details' about yourself such as post code (again), DOB, mobile number and double check you're definitely the gender you think you are
- Tell them how many people live in your household and choose from an endless list of dietary requirements
- Request a card
- Wait around for the card to turn up
- Sign back into your account
- Try to remember your memorable password
- Enter your 19 digit card number onto the website
- Then enter the CORRECT 19 digit card number
- Realise the price match difference is given to you in points
- Learn that 1p = 10 points
- Then realise you can only start saving when you have your first 5,000 points
- Practise your mental arithmetic and work out that 5,000 points is £5
- Go into your M local store and discover you can't use your loyalty card here
- Head to a big Morrisons
- Find out your basket must include one product that is comparable to another supermarket's to make a saving
- Pick up some beans and realise they aren't part of the deal
- Try and find the beans that are part of the deal
- Wonder if that applies to beans with sausages?
- Search for other applicable items so your shop exceeds the £15 required spend
- Finally, receive your £5 voucher after you've paid for your stuff
- Get told you can only spend the £5 voucher on your next shop

Or you could just go to

©Lidl

This ad was run in the UK by supermarket chain Lidl, in response to a price-matching offer by its competitor, Morrisons.

Beautiful, isn't it?

Effective ads need no explanation – and this one is no exception. Nevertheless, I think it's worth considering why it is so good.

# 1. IT DEMONSTRATES THE BENEFIT

The premise of this ad – that shopping at Lidl is both economical and convenient – is not simply stated but actively demonstrated. Merely reading about the process for taking up Morrisons' price-matching offer (let alone actually going through with it) makes you feel exhausted. This is no accident.

# 2. IT'S A DIRECTLY COMPETITIVE AD FOR A GOOD REASON

It's well known that competitive advertising is fraught with danger, because calling out your competitor runs the risk of giving them free publicity. But as with all the best competitive ads – still exemplified by the classic Avis 'We try harder' campaign – there is a clear strategy behind it here. The competitor's price-match offer is shown up (and how!) as a weak proposition.

What's more, the advertisers have clearly done their research about exactly why this is so. And even if they have embellished the onerous nature of the process for customers, they have made it plausible enough to be persuasive.

# 3. IT SPEAKS THE LANGUAGE OF HUMANS

You'll notice that there is not one mention of 'innovation' here. There's no 'passion' either. No 'commitment'. In fact, there is none of the clichéd, pretentious guff that you see in most ads these days. What's more – and we're getting into hen's teeth territory now – the ad actually has some charm. A bit of understated wit, without descending into that utterly unfunny, self-regarding, hipster-driven nonsense that's now so prevalent in advertising.

# 4. NOTHING GETS IN THE WAY OF THE IDEA

This ad could so easily have gone pear-shaped. Someone could have insisted on including a banal photo of a smiling supermarket worker, or on reducing the length of the copy, or on making the logo bigger. So while the copywriter should be given a round of applause, the art director and client are equally deserving of credit. The art direction here, while deceptively simple, is superb. And the client has been brave enough not to compromise a strong idea with advertising clichés.

# 5. IT'S A SOCIAL MEDIA SUCCESS WITHOUT BEING A LOAD OF ####

This ad was quite a hit on social media. While not quite 'trending', perhaps, it was widely shared on Twitter. But unlike some of the so-called responsive advertising that receives plaudits on social media – much of which is inane gimmickry, if you ask me – this is not a 'social media ad'. With the exception of a highway billboard, perhaps, this ad would work in just about any medium. Indeed, it echoes some of the great print ads of the past.

So in summary, this is a good idea that has been carefully crafted. If it works like a charm (and wins awards), it will be Lidl wonder.

# THE ARTICLE YOU'LL NEVER SEE

[An interview with the
ECD of a Major Agency]

**INTERVIEWER:**

**What are your plans this year?
Will you be looking to create game-
changing social trends that redefine
the role of agencies and challenge
traditional industry assumptions?**

ECD:

Nah, we're just going to make some ads.

# THE TEMPLATE FOR EVERY MEN'S WATCH AD

---

**PICTURE OF WATCH**

---

**AN APPEAL TO THE MALE EGO**

A non sequitur

---

Some crap about astronauts or pilots

**LOGO**

# WHAT KIND OF AGENCY PERSON ARE YOU?

Would you rather plan work than do work?

**YES** → YOU ARE A STRATEGIST

**NO** → Is your work creative?

**NO** → YOU ARE A SUIT

**YES** → Do other people take credit for it?

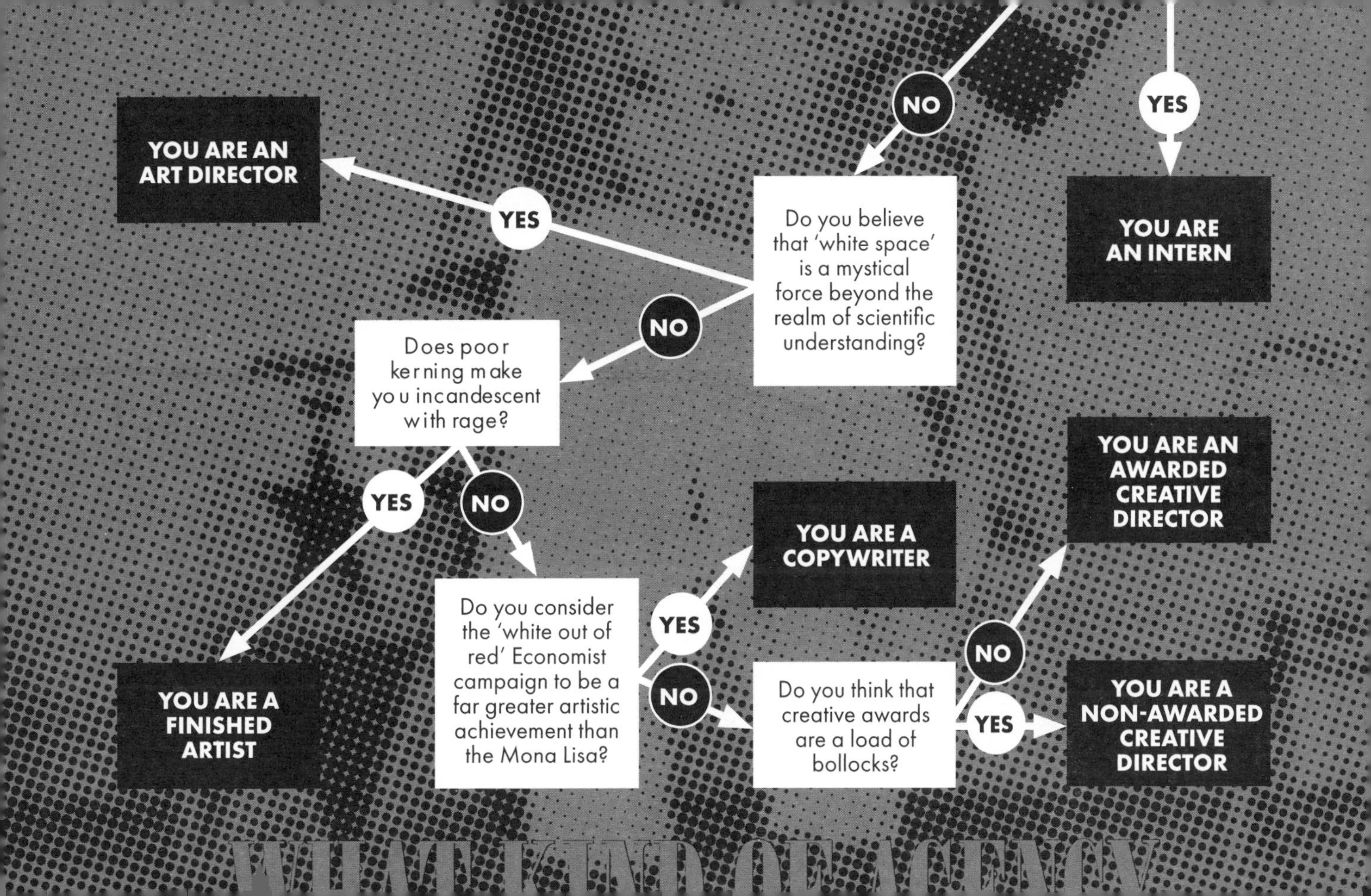

NO
YES
YOU ARE AN INTERN
Do you believe that 'white space' is a mystical force beyond the realm of scientific understanding?
YES
YOU ARE AN ART DIRECTOR
NO
Does poor kerning make you incandescent with rage?
YES
YOU ARE A FINISHED ARTIST
NO
Do you consider the 'white out of red' Economist campaign to be a far greater artistic achievement than the Mona Lisa?
YES
YOU ARE A COPYWRITER
NO
Do you think that creative awards are a load of bollocks?
NO
YOU ARE AN AWARDED CREATIVE DIRECTOR
YES
YOU ARE A NON-AWARDED CREATIVE DIRECTOR

IF THE CLASSIC, 'LEMON' AD WERE WRITTEN TODAY

©Volkswagen

# Experience optimal quality.

At Volkswagen, we are passionate about perfection.
That's why we go the extra mile to ensure delivery of innovative
vehicular solutions that align with our company vision to add
value in everything we do. It's all about moving forward.

Because Volkswagen is not a car. It's a journey - our journey.

Join the conversation at optimalquality.com

CREATIVITY

# THE CULT OF CREATIVITY

**W**hen I was about 15, I got pretty heavily into The Cult.

No, I don't mean I fell under the influence of some dodgy guru who spouted pseudo-spiritual platitudes and fleeced his followers out of their life savings. In fact I didn't encounter any dudes like that until much later, when I joined 'marketing Twitter'.

(Sorry.)

In this instance, The Cult I'm referring to is the English band of the '80s and '90s.

The album that got me into The Cult was Sonic Temple – something of a modern classic, in my opinion. Right from its distinctive opening riffs, Sonic Temple is a rollicking rock masterpiece with nary a bad track on it.

Come to think of it, maybe my infatuation with The Cult was a little cult-like after all. You see, I was so impressed with Sonic Temple that I decided to spend my life savings to that point (which must have been at least $85) on The Cult's earlier albums. And that's when things went a bit pear-shaped.

Without even giving it a precautionary listen, I bought their debut, Dreamtime. And it's fair to say I was a touch disappointed. By which I mean I felt like vomiting.

I swear I tried to give Dreamtime a decent hearing. But ultimately I decided it was a load of hot garbage.

That's probably harsh in hindsight, and of course these things are inherently subjective. Nonetheless, I think you'd struggle to find many people (excluding all those impeccably hirsute 'I knew that band before they were popular' hipst/los-ers) who would rate Dreamtime anywhere near as highly as Sonic Temple.

Reflecting on it now, there's something quite reassuring about that, because it lays bare the truth of the typical creative process.

Creativity is sometimes idealised in popular culture, in that we like to think of it as a revelatory event. Once the muse strikes, the outcome is essentially a *fait accompli*.

After all, Dolly Parton famously wrote 'Jolene' and 'I Will Always Love You' on the same day.

The same. Freaking. Day.

And Paul McCartney literally created 'Yesterday' overnight, after the melody came to him in a dream. Not too bad for the most covered song of all time.

On that point, it's certainly true that sleep can be good for unlocking subconscious ideas, as demonstrated by (shameless plug alert) my advice on how to be creative (see opposite).

So don't get me wrong. There's no doubt that creativity can sometimes be spontaneous – maybe even instantaneous – but the reality of creative work tends to be a lot more prosaic.

Like most artists, The Cult didn't achieve brilliance from the outset. Hell, they barely achieved mediocrity.

But they got to brilliance in the end – and their path to it was characterised by steady improvement. In my opinion, every album along the way was an upgrade on its predecessor.

Not to draw too long a bow, but The Cult's career progression might be considered a microcosm of the creative process in general.

To my ears, those early albums were a bit like a writer's first drafts: inconsistent, unpolished and basically all over the place. The difference, of course, is that their 'drafts' were exposed to the full glare of the public domain.

At this point I'm almost inclined

to think 'those poor buggers', but I suspect they can console themselves by frolicking in their piles of cash (which is more than you can say for most of us writers).

And in any event, there's an even more brutal example of being publicly judged for one's creative work. Because if musicians have it tough in terms of audience criticism, then stand-up comedians arguably have it worse.

I can't think of many situations that would be more humiliating than doing stand-up comedy and 'dying' on stage in front of hundreds of people. (Well, to be fair, I can think of quite a few but they're not fit for publication here. Try Urban Dictionary if you really want to know.)

While 'dying' on stage must be awful, 'killing' a stand-up set would surely be an exhilarating experience.

But here's the thing. The difference between dying and killing in stand-up comedy can simply be a matter of time and timing.

From what I understand, it takes time to discover what works and what doesn't in stand-up comedy – and sometimes this can come down to seemingly minuscule changes in the timing of one's delivery. So it's a process of constant refinement, and its practitioners tend to be utterly pedantic in the way they hone their routines.

I think there's a lesson in that for all of us who work in creative industries – namely, that the creative process can be a hard slog. Sure, there will be occasions when inspiration will hit you like lightning, but most of the time you'll just need to trudge your way through the storm.

Don't believe any gurus who tell you otherwise.

# HOW TO BE CREATIVE

Define the problem that you need to solve.

Stare out of the window.

Take a break.

Stare at a computer screen.

Go outside for a change of scene.

Stare at a blank notebook.

Go to bed.

Stare at the ceiling.

Just as you're drifting off, have the most extraordinarily brilliant idea in the history of humanity.

Wake up with no recollection of the idea.

# CREATIVE AGENCY PLAYLIST

orking 5 to 9, what a way to make a living'

'Time(sheet) after time(sheet)'

9 problems and a pitch is at least 84 of them'

n't believe the (trendy new platform) hype'

spirit – or certainly no older than mid-twenties spirit'

'Ch-ch-ch-changes'

und what I'm looking for in this fucking image library'

/ Just killed the plan / Put a pun in there instead
/ Make the logo bigger, client said'

Anything by Cut Copy

are digitally remastered, because digital is always better.

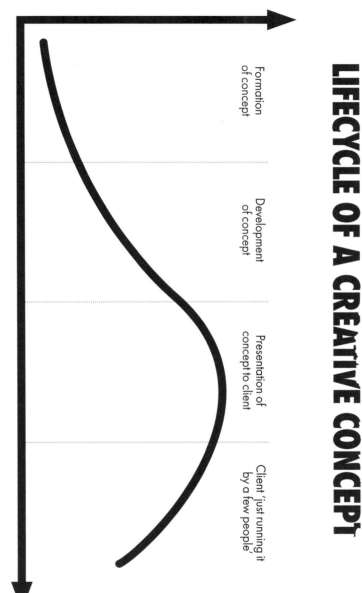

**PROBABILITY OF SURVIVAL**

**TIME**

# LIFECYCLE OF A CREATIVE CONCEPT

Formation of concept

Development of concept

Presentation of concept to client

Client 'just running it by a few people'

# BACH TO THE FUTURE: THE COMPOSTING OF CREATIVITY

A little while ago, on the increasingly toxic psychological dumpster-fire that is Twitter, someone shared a timely timeline cleanser. Taken from an interview with Paul Simon, it's several minutes of brilliance that I implore you to watch: (Google 'Paul Simon writing process for Bridge Over Troubled Water').

# ROLE
# TION IN

Aside from being a lovely musical demonstration, this video also serves as a superb example of the creative process more broadly.

Personally, I had no idea that Bridge Over Troubled Water drew on so many, shall we say, inspirations. There is certainly nothing inherent in the song that makes them obvious – and nor would you suspect that they come from such varied sources. The finished product sounds seamless and original (or at least it does to my unsophisticated ears).

And that, I think, gets to the heart of the matter – that creativity is often a process of making links between disparate influences to synthesise something new.

Another good example of this is one of my favourite artists: Girl Talk. If you're not familiar with Girl Talk, all I can say is I feel sorry for you and strongly encourage you to rectify this situation – it will make your life 35% more fun.

Shameless fanboy-ing aside, let me explain why this example is relevant.

Girl Talk (aka Gregg Gillis) is a DJ/producer who specialises in mashups of other artists' tracks. To give you an idea of just how many sources he uses in his compositions – and how eclectic they are – look up the data visualisation of his 'All Day' album. You can click on the individual bars to see the details of each track.

To me, the really impressive part about this album is that it doesn't sound like a fragmented hodgepodge – it's a coherent piece of work that is quite different from its constituent parts. To wit, when I now hear the component songs on their own, I find myself half-expecting a bass drop or an Ice Cube lyric that never comes – because it wasn't on the original track.

# In other words, the work is simultaneously familiar and new.

And of course, there are examples of this in advertising too. Such as this famous ad by David Ogilvy (see opposite).

That headline was lifted, word for word, from an earlier one for the Pierce-Arrow car.

Amateurs imagine original, quirky approaches work best. Not so: what matters is to say the right thing. Something that promises a strong benefit or escape from something people dislike.

And by the way, those previous two paragraphs aren't mine – I stole them verbatim from an article by Drayton Bird.

The Rolls-Royce Silver Cloud—$13,995

## "At 60 miles an hour the loudest noise in this new Rolls-Royce comes from the electric clock"

*What makes Rolls-Royce the best car in the world? "There is really no magic about it—it is merely patient attention to detail," says an eminent Rolls-Royce engineer.*

1. "At 60 miles an hour the loudest noise comes from the electric clock," reports the Technical Editor of THE MOTOR. Three mufflers tune out sound frequencies—acoustically.

2. Every Rolls-Royce engine is run for seven hours at full throttle before installation, and each car is test-driven for hundreds of miles over varying road surfaces.

3. The Rolls-Royce is designed as an *owner-driven* car. It is eighteen inches shorter than the largest domestic cars.

4. The car has power steering, power brakes and automatic gear-shift. It is very easy to drive and to park. No chauffeur required.

5. The finished car spends a week in the final test-shop, being fine-tuned. Here it is subjected to 98 separate ordeals. For example, the engineers use a *stethoscope* to listen for axle-whine.

6. The Rolls-Royce is guaranteed for *three*

years. With a new network of dealers and parts-depots from Coast to Coast, service is no problem.

7. The Rolls-Royce radiator has never changed, except that when Sir Henry Royce died in 1933 the monogram RR was changed from red to black.

8. The coachwork is given five coats of primer paint, and hand rubbed between each coat, before *nine* coats of finishing paint go on.

9. By moving a switch on the steering column, you can adjust the shock-absorbers to suit road conditions.

10. A picnic table, veneered in French walnut, slides out from under the dash. Two more swing out behind the front seats.

11. You can get such optional extras as an Espresso coffee-making machine, a dictating machine, a bed, hot and cold water for washing, an electric razor or a telephone.

12. There are three separate systems of power brakes, two hydraulic and one mechanical. Damage to one system will not affect the others. The Rolls-Royce is a very *safe* car—and also a very *lively* car. It cruises serenely at eighty-five. Top speed is in excess of 100 m.p.h.

13. The Bentley is made by Rolls-Royce. Except for the radiators, they are identical motor cars, manufactured by the same engineers in the same works. People who feel diffident about driving a Rolls-Royce can buy a Bentley.

PRICE. The Rolls-Royce illustrated in this advertisement—f.o.b. principal ports of entry—costs **$13,995.**

If you would like the rewarding experience of driving a Rolls-Royce or Bentley, write or telephone to one of the dealers listed on the opposite page.

Rolls-Royce Inc., 10 Rockefeller Plaza, New York 20, N. Y., Circle 5-1144.

March 1959

As Drayton alludes to in that article, our industry's obsession with originality is myopic.

If Paul Simon can use a Bach melody, surely we can draw some inspiration from the advertising of the past. Bach lived more than 200 years ago (which roughly equates to a millennium in ad agency years) – yet some people in advertising eschew influences that are even 20 years old, let alone 200.

There are many examples of brilliant work from the earlier days of advertising, of course, so ignoring it due to a misguided pursuit of originality is downright silly.

Imagine if physicists deliberately avoided building on the work of Newton or Einstein, for the sake of being original. Advertising isn't physics, to state the ridiculously obvious, but the principle is relevant nevertheless.

To use another scientific analogy, creativity is more often a process of inheritance than a *de novo* event. The magic lies in the transformation of what is inherited – so that what's old becomes new again (to steal a line from Stephen King).

As Pablo Picasso – who was no Girl Talk, but still a pretty decent artist – famously said: 'Good artists copy, great artists steal.'

IMAGINE IF PHYSICISTS DELIBERATELY AVOIDED BUILDING ON THE WORK OF NEWTON OR EINSTEIN, FOR THE SAKE OF BEING ORIGINAL.

# THINGS YOU SHOULD NEVER SAY TO A DESIGNER

It's all done. I just need you to make it look pretty.

Can you design it in Word?

Please use Comic Sans.

Make it pop.

I'm not a designer, but...

It won't take long – just put the new copy into last year's design.

Tszuj it up a bit.

But I can get 50 logos for that price on Fiverr.

Can you make 400 words fit in a quarter-page ad?

My boss/spouse/toddler doesn't like your choice of font/colour/career.

Move the image to the left. A bit further. No, not that far. *[Image back to original position]* Perfect!

# THE FORMULA FOR BULLSHIT

$$B = (ctG\textstyle\sum)^{SF}/u$$

**Where:**

**B** is the bullshit quotient

**c** is the unnecessary complexity of the idea being expressed

**t** is the number of 'thought leaders' who came up with the idea

**G** is the gullibility of the industry to which it applies

**$\sum$** is a random mathematical symbol included purely to confuse people

**SF** is the 'social factor': the extent to which the idea is mindlessly regurgitated on social media

**u** is the utility of the idea to anyone other than the people making a shitload of money from it

DUCK HUNTING:
DUCK HUNTING:
DUCK HUNTING:

# DUCK HUNTING: THE AGENCY VERSION

Four people from a creative agency went duck hunting one day: a strategist, an art director, a copywriter and an account manager.

Before long, a bird came flying overhead. The first to react was the strategist, who raised his shotgun but then hesitated. 'Before we do anything else,' he said, 'I think we need to define exactly what a duck is.' And by that time, the bird was long gone.

Soon after, another bird appeared. The art director saw this one, but she was reluctant to act too. 'We're not shooting anything until the conditions are right and the light is perfect,' she muttered, as the creature flew off.

The next person to see a bird was the copywriter. She was confident about its identity, but paused for a moment and said: 'That's definitely a duck, but do we really need to shoot it? Maybe it would be better if we just describe its features.' While she wrestled with this dilemma, the bird disappeared.

Finally, the account manager saw a bird fly overhead. Without the slightest hesitation, he blasted it out of the sky. 'I don't care what that was,' he said. 'I'm taking it to the client in half an hour and you guys are going to convince them it's a duck.'

WE DEMAND THAT YOU PITCH YOUR CREATIVE IDEAS FOR FREE.
AND ACCEPT PERFORMANCE-BASED PAYMENT.
AND INCREASE YOUR DIVERSITY.
ALSO, MAKE THE LOGO BIGGER.

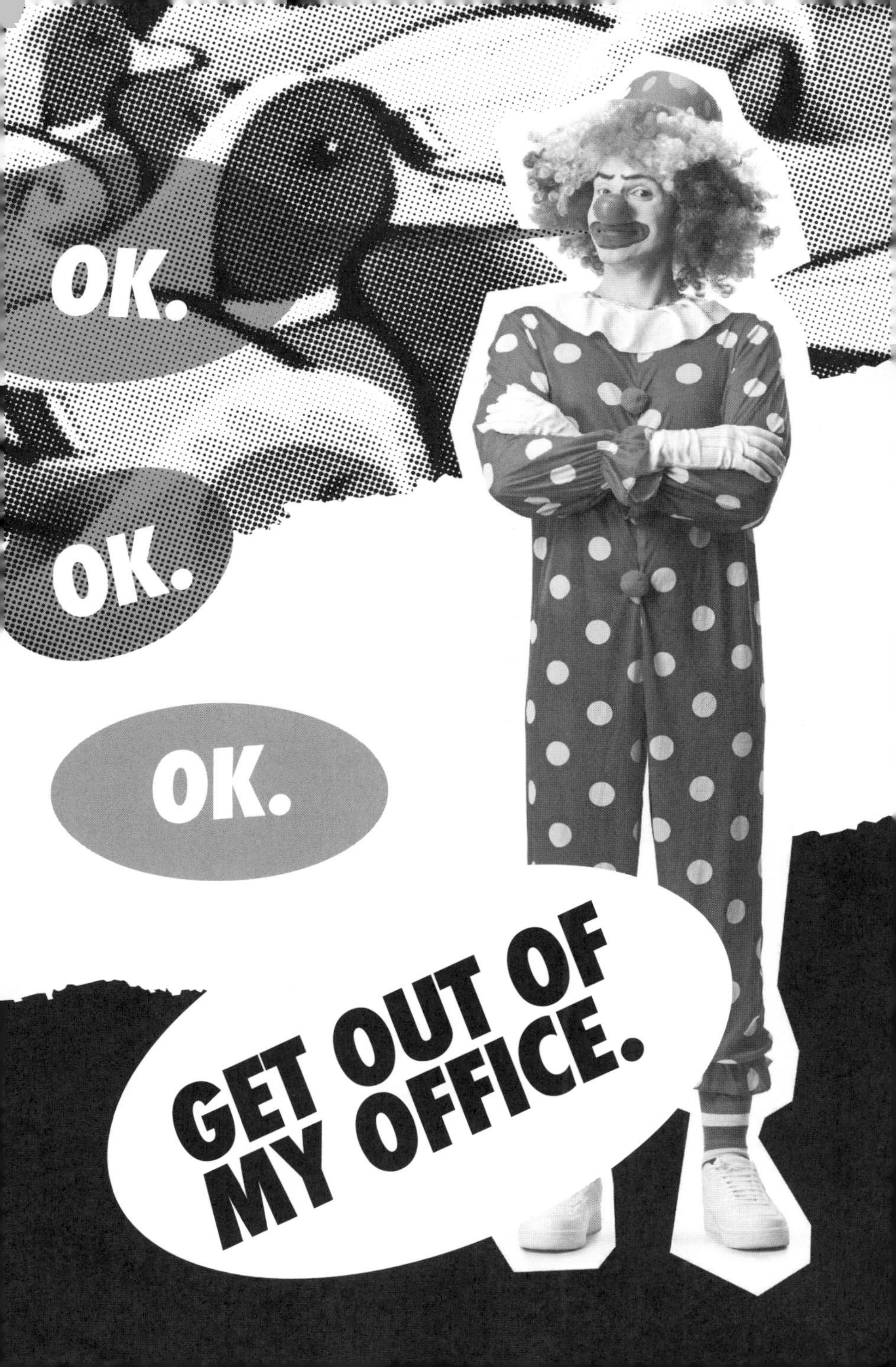
OK.
OK.
OK.
GET OUT OF
MY OFFICE.

# IN THEORY

**INNOVATION IS AN IMPORTANT CONSIDERATION FOR AGENCIES.**

**ADVERTISING NEEDS NON-CONFORMISTS.**

**BRAINSTORMS ARE GREAT FOR GENERATING CREATIVE IDEAS.**

**CREATIVE WORK MUST ALWAYS BE INFORMED BY STRATEGY.**

**GOOD IDEAS CAN COME FROM ANYONE.**

**DIVERSITY IS A PRIORITY FOR CREATIVE AGENCIES.**

# IN PRACTICE

**INNOVATION IS AN IMPORTANT BUZZWORD FOR AGENCIES.**

**BLACK SHIRTS AND FOLDED ARMS. NO EXCEPTIONS.**

**BRAINSTORMS ARE GREAT FOR GENERATING WHITEBOARDS FULL OF INDECIPHERABLE BOLLOCKS.**

**'WE NEED A 6-SECOND VIRAL VIDEO BY CLOSE OF BUSINESS TODAY. BECAUSE AGILE.'**

**NAH.**

**IF YOU'RE NOT A 23 YEAR-OLD TIKTOK INFLUENCER CALLED TOM, THEN FUCK OFF.**

# INSTRUCTIONS FOR WORKING WITH CREATIVES

1. First, go through rigorous interviews with the GCD, ECD, CCO, CEO and anyone else with a TLA.

2. Then complete a personality test. This will label you with a highly specific personality type, albeit with the scientific validity of a horoscope written in excrement by a medieval witch.

3. Conform to our homogenous culture.

4. Ensure that everything you do, no matter how inconsequential, is entered into our project-management platform.

**5.** The exception to this is time expended on jobs, as that needs to be entered into our timesheet platform (in 3-minute increments).

**6.** Oh, and there's also another platform for communicating with colleagues. No, you can't just go and 'talk' to them – what year do you think this is?

**7.** Sit through meetings that involve a minimum of 80 slides. At least half of these slides will feature incomprehensible graphs.

**8.** Adhere to an endless list of legal and regulatory requirements.

**9.** Wear a metaphorical straitjacket. Never do work that differs from what we're used to seeing.

**10.** Now go and be creative – just have fun with it!

# A TYPICAL REQUEST AT A CREATIVE AGENCY

'We want to do a stunt that gets the whole world talking, like the Tesla in space thing.

Budget is 5K.'

# IF PEOPLE IN AD AGENCIES HAD THEIR OWN TAGLINES

**Account Directors**
The deadline is tomorrow

**Strategists**
Technically, that's not an insight

**Creative Directors**
It's been done

**Copywriters**
Can I add some copy?

**Art Directors**
Can you delete some copy?

**Social Media Managers**
ok boomer tiktok lol

# THE GOLDILOCKS ZONE OF CREATIVITY

**M**y daughter has a subscription to the National Geographic Kids magazine.

Before you ask, no, I'm definitely not one of those parents who force their kids to read nerdy stuff rather than watch mindless nonsense on YouTube.

(For the record, though, some of it really is mindless nonsense. Christ alive.)

The truth is that my daughter just loves reading about animals. In fact she kind of loses interest once it gets to the vegetable and mineral stuff, which makes me think the subscription might be slightly wasted on her.

Anyway, we were reading the magazine the other day, and we came across a piece about the 'Goldilocks zone'.

Obviously I was already well versed in this astronomical concept (ahem) but in case you haven't heard of it before, the Goldilocks zone is the distance of a planet from its star that enables the right temperature for water to remain liquid on the planet's surface.

If its star is too far away, the planet gets too cold (i.e. the water freezes) and if its star is too close, the planet gets too hot (so the water boils away).

But if the planet is the right distance from its star (like the Earth is from our sun), then the temperature is just right for water to remain liquid. And as far as we know, liquid water is an essential ingredient for life – which is why the Goldilocks zone is also known as the habitable zone.

Like me, the term 'Goldilocks zone' originated in the 1970s.

Also like me, it needs the conditions to be just right before life is possible.

To come to life each morning, I need eight hours of uninterrupted sleep. Then three coffees, give or take. And finally a quick bump of coke. (I'm joking, of course – as if a father of young kids would ever get eight hours of uninterrupted sleep.)

After I came to life today, it struck me that there is a kind of Goldilocks zone for creativity. Let's call it the 'creativity zone', because that's the most creative name I can come up with right now. Suffice it to say I could really do with some c... er, coffee.

My 'creativity zone' theory is predicated on the idea that certain conditions must be met before creativity is possible.

For example, if you are too far removed from sources of inspiration, creativity is nigh-on impossible. After all, most creative work draws on and puts together various elements from external influences. 'Everything is a remix', as they say.

This is why it's so important for creatives to keep proximity to varied sources of inspiration. We need to listen, read, observe, take note, and let it all percolate.

These inputs might not necessarily do much – they might sit in your head like cerebral space junk, as it were – but if you have them in your orbit (well, a bit behind the orbit, anatomically speaking), one day your brain might make a connection that's 'just right'.

I came across a great example of this on Twitter the other day – a clip that shows how Damon Albarn used a preset melody from an 80s synth machine to create the introductory hook to the Gorillaz' hit 'Clint Eastwood'.

Who would have thought, huh? You just never know where inspiration might come from.

But conversely, it's possible to get too close to sources of inspiration. I think we see this a lot in advertising – particularly when it comes to following industry trends.

Look at the way advertising has evolved over recent decades and this becomes pretty obvious.

The serif fonts. Then the sans serif fonts. Then the sans legibility fonts.

The long copy. Then the short copy. Then the complete disdain for copy.

Now we have the seemingly ubiquitous use of 'Reimagined' and 'Reinvented' and 'Redefined'. The 'ads for ad people'. And of course the ads for non-existent social causes, which only ever ran once in the Republic of Iranascam.

The fact is that an awful lot of advertising seems to draw its inspiration from other advertising, rather than from broader contexts. Which means it all becomes a bit of a circle-j... er, navel-gazing exercise.

So, to sum up my theory: if you're too far away from sources of inspiration, your creative output will freeze up; but if you're too close to them, you'll just create hot air.

Or in case you want a more visual representation, I've made this handy illustration, below (please excuse the technical jargon).

So my advice is to look around for creative inspiration, but don't get blinded by what's closest to you. And once you've soaked it all up, sleep on it – for that's when creativity works its celestial magic. The journalist Miles Kington might just as well have been talking about creatives when he said: 'Astronomers, like burglars and jazz musicians, operate best at night.'

## THE CREATIVITY ZONE

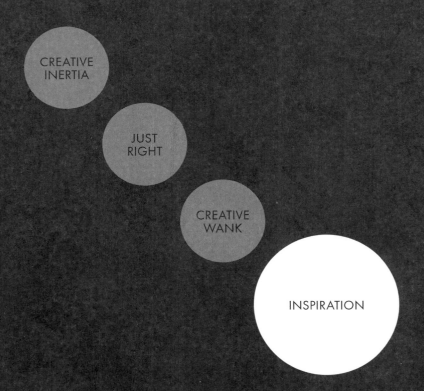

CREATIVE
INERTIA

JUST
RIGHT

CREATIVE
WANK

INSPIRATION

BUSINESS

5 WAYS 5 WAYS
5 WAYS 5 WAYS
5 WAYS 5 WAYS

# 5 WAYS
# THAT BIG DATA
# WILL CHANGE
# YOUR LIFE

1. With big data, you no longer need to make decisions. By the time you've sorted through all that data, the opportunity to do anything useful with it will be long gone.

2. You will adore all the advertising you see. No more of that untargeted, relatively unobtrusive crap. Thanks to big data, you'll get ads that know you intimately, follow you around obsessively, and invade your space at every opportunity like a mob of unhinged online stalkers. Who doesn't want that?

3. You can put creatives in their place. Whenever they present you with a creative idea, shut it down immediately by simply saying 'Explain to me how this is big-data-driven'. Numbers are like kryptonite to those hippies.

4. Big data allows you to do whatever the hell you want. Let's say you collect some data that doesn't support your argument. No problem; just go get some more data that does. The beauty of big data is not the data – it's the bigness.

5. You now have an immediate answer for any business question. Someone asks what your strategy is? Big data. A client asks how you're going to increase their sales? Big data. Some idiot wants to know what the fuck big data is exactly? It's big data. Idiot.

# THE 15-SECOND MBA

1. A loud voice always compensates far a lack of knowledge.

2. All it takes to make something a science is to call it a science.

3. Never use one buzzword when you can use 50.

4. No matter how experienced or qualified someone is in their field of expertise, you know more than they do.

5. Don't 'do' what you can talk about instead.

6. There is no concept so complex that It can't be reduced to a 2x2 matrix.

7. There is no concept so simple that it can't be drawn out to a 250-page report.

8. No matter what you get paid, you deserve more.

9. You can turn around any business simply by thinking about it for a couple of hours.

10. Self-doubt is for losers.

EVERY
EVERY

# EVERY CONSULTING FIRM'S CONSUMER SURVEY REPORT

- 88% of consumers would pay more for a brand that has a worthy social purpose. Well, they say they would – and that's what really matters.

- When asked a ridiculously leading question designed to elicit a response consistent with our vested interests, almost everyone answered in the way we wanted them to.

- For example, 96% of respondents said they would rather buy a sustainable product than kill a puppy.

- Young people are concerned about housing affordability. This kind of searing insight explains why we make the big bucks.

- Most young people also think that society is becoming more altruistic. Bless.

- 60% of respondents said the pandemic has given them a sense that we're all in this together. This is actually a verbatim finding from a Deloitte survey – I kid you not.

- Today's consumers are more likely to buy products that are manufactured ethically. Admittedly, the control group for this analysis was a carefully chosen assortment of criminal psychopaths.

- 100% of our survey respondents said they never watch 'adult entertainment'. We briefly considered the possibility that this might call into question the veracity of their other responses, but we dismissed it on the basis that this survey makes us a fucktonne of money.

WHY DID THE MARKETER CROSS THE ROAD?

BECAUSE SIMON SAID.

| TITLE | WHAT IT MEANS |
| --- | --- |
| Chief Executive Officer | Manager |
| Chief Operating Officer | Manager's golf buddy |
| Chief Financial Officer | Bookkeeper |
| Chief Information Officer | IT support |
| Chief Strategy Officer | Person who plans stuff |
| Chief Innovation Officer | Person who talks about planning stuff |
| Chief Creative Officer | Amateur musician |
| Chief Customer Officer | God only knows |

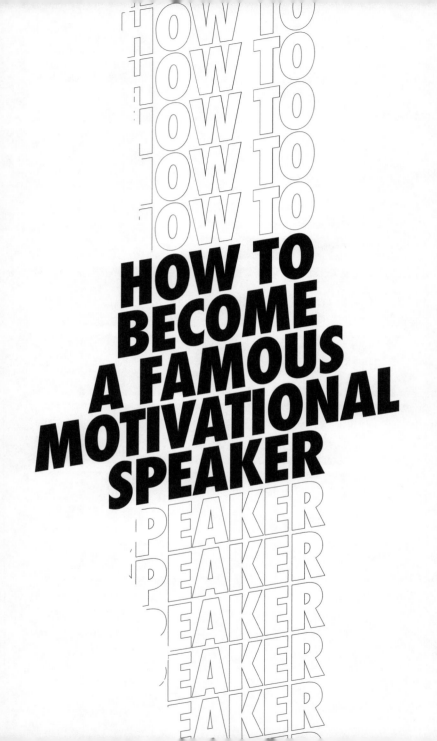

1. First of all, you need to be male. And not just any male, either. You need to be a hyper-fucko-mega-male.

2. To fully signal your testosteronal awesomeness, you must ensure that your jaw is at least twice the width of your head. And don't let anybody tell you that this is impossible because of your 'genes' or 'biology' – the prominence of your jawline is directly proportional to how hard you hustle.

3. Shout at all times. Speaking at a comfortably audible volume is a sign of weakness.

4. Your goal is to inspire people to be successful. The first step in this process is to tell them they are abject failures who are doing everything wrong.

5. Now that you've endeared yourself to your audience, the next step is to explain how they can turn their pathetic lives around. This is quite simple. Just stand in the middle of the auditorium, beat your chest like an amphetamine-fuelled silverback gorilla and scream 'JUST BE LIKE ME, YOU FUCKING LOSERS'.

6. When you get caught out for saying something incredibly stupid about women – which is inevitable, given that you'll say something incredibly stupid about every topic – simply apologise unreservedly. Nah, just kidding! Make the apology all about YOU.

7. At no point should you provide any sensible advice that your audience might learn from. If you're going to keep selling your snake oil, you need to keep those suckers stupid.

It was a Monday morning. I had just finished my weekly meditation session with the Dalai Lama and was on my way to a meeting with Jeff Bezos.

That was when I noticed a dishevelled young man, shivering by the side of the road.

With the compassion that I am renowned for, I asked him if he was OK. He said it was the first time any human had ever spoken to him, and broke down in tears of gratitude.

I would have given him my monogrammed $3,000 Louis Vuitton handkerchief, but I knew that would be a crass way of demonstrating the gulf between us. So I fished a used tissue out of the gutter and gently offered that to him instead.

He gave me a weak smile, as if to say: 'You're an incredibly important alpha male who has much better things to do'. I nodded grudgingly in agreement.

But I wasn't just going to leave him there. So I gave him a ride to the local soup kitchen in my convertible Maserati. As we parted, he said it was the greatest day of his life.

Remember, even if you become insanely successful like me, don't forget the little people like, er, I forget his name now.

# THE OFFICE OLYMPICS

## Marathon
A meeting that goes on for several hours, is gruelling for all involved, and occasionally leads to incontinence.

## Sprint
A frantic race to meet the deadline for a written document. Often slowed down by track changes.

## Discus
A discussion that is cut short, usually because the boss has just walked in.

## Synchronised skimming
When two colleagues simultaneously speed-read a report for a meeting they had completely forgotten about.

## Decaflon
Having to complete one's professional duties without the assistance of caffeine. Can be dangerous for bystanders.

## Cable tennis
The process of switching back and forth between different cables in a futile attempt to connect to a projector for a vitally important presentation.

## Mental gymnastics
A demonstration of extraordinary cognitive skill, in which a co-worker is able to convince themselves that your idea was actually theirs.

# MAKING A DIFFERENCE! NOW.

**O**n the off chance that you haven't noticed, everyone is making a difference these days.

Just last weekend, in a single newspaper, I saw no fewer than five instances of organisations claiming to 'make a difference'.

Even several years ago, 'Making a difference' was already a hackneyed expression, especially in healthcare communications.

And yet it seems that many people are unaware of the faintly ludicrous status of this phrase, for it continues to be ubiquitous.

Hospital ads, school ads, job ads, you name it. You'd think it was illegal for any organisation with so much as a vaguely altruistic purpose not to assert how much difference it's making.

Now, to be fair, 'making a difference' probably started off quite innocently – and it is, after all, an honourable sentiment.

It's simple but emotive, with a rallying quality. And it genuinely describes the function of most healthcare providers, educators and charities. They can and do make a difference to people's lives.

But there really can be too much of a good thing when it comes to language like this.

It doesn't take long for a worthy sentiment to become an infuriating cliché. Someone sees it somewhere, likes the

sound of it, mentions it at a meeting, adopts it for their own organisation, and on it goes.

So the irony is that what may well be a credible claim appears disingenuous, if not outright dishonest.

Can all these difference-makers really be making such a difference? If their tired and, frankly, lazy choice of language is any guide, you have to wonder whether they would be sufficiently 'committed' (to use another awful cliché) to make any difference at all.

And another problem with 'making a difference' is differentiation – or rather the lack of it. When everyone is saying the same thing, everyone seems the same. Any genuine differences get lost in a blancmange of indistinguishable platitudes.

So my advice is to stop saying you make a difference. It will make a difference to your communications.

But in case you need any reminding, just refer to this handy algorithm.

# UPDATED SAYINGS FOR THE DIGITAL ERA

I thinkfluence, therefore I am.

The user journey of a thousand
miles begins with a single click.

Real-time waits for no man.

Now is the winter of our dissed content.

Seize the data.

2D or not 2D, that is the question.

A man's tweet is as good as his bitcoin.

If music be the food of love,
illegally download it.

Nothing in the world can take the place of
persisten... ah fuck it, I'm not reading all that.

# IF COMPANY DEPARTMENTS WERE ASKED: 'WHAT MAKES A RAINBOW BEAUTIFUL?'

**Marketing:** 'A rainbow is beautiful if the people looking at it believe it's beautiful'

**Business development:** 'Look, we wouldn't even be having this discussion if I wasn't making rain'

**Accounts:** 'What makes a rainbow beautiful is less important than how that beauty depreciates in a pre-determined manner over time'

**Procurement:** 'The rainbow's beauty is irrelevant – all that matters is what I have to give up to see it'

**Sales:** 'If people believe a rainbow is beautiful, that's because I've been out there telling them it's beautiful'

**Legal:** 'What? It's raining? We need to check the status of our umbrellas'

**IT:** 'There shouldn't be a rainbow at all these days. Only the Cloud'

**The CEO:** 'Who cares about the fucking rainbow? Just show me the pot of gold'

# I MAKE $2 MILLION/MONTH IN REVENUE. IN A BAD MONTH.

Here are the 5 websites that enable my outrageous success.

## UnqualifiedLeads.com
Marketing is easy and requires no expertise whatsoever.
This site will remove any doubts you may have about that.

## ChatWank.com
Want to become a ChatGPT expert? This training module, written by
ChatGPT of course, will have you fully qualified in a matter of minutes.

## AbsoluteGrifter.org
This is an amazing resource if you have limitless ambition but zero talent.

## CopyCharlatans.com
Anyone can be a copywriter, as this terribly written website proves.

## Narcissists.com
Whenever I doubt myself, this is my go-to. I'm instantly among peers,
albeit slightly inferior ones.

# THE INNOVATIONS THAT WE REALLY NEED

### Artificial vacuity (AV)
A technology that will make certain roles redundant, such as those of Instagram influencers, the Kardashian family, and social media CEOs.

### Unblockchain
A sophisticated database that allows people to verify the precise location of a plumber at any given time. Thanks to this revolutionary technology, customers will no longer be forced to wait 3 days for a tradesman who never arrives.

### Analogue transformation
The process by which a company eliminates all of its digital systems, such as email, intranet and Slack. Analogue transformation has been shown to increase productivity by 260%.

### Storykilling
An application that automatically mutes any word beginning with 'story' such as storytelling, storydoing, storymaking or storyliving.

### Antisocial media
Oh, sorry. LinkedIn already exists.

2020 has been a hard year for a lot of people.

But not for me! I've been absolutely crushing it all year.

Now, I understand that some of you may not want to hear about my outrageous success when you've been doing it tough. But to that I say: have a little empathy, for crying out loud. Try to put yourself in my $30,000 Testoni dress shoes (for which I must thank myself for winning an amazing new client!).

The year started as it usually does, with dozens of projects that I was killing without mercy. But then the pandemic hit, and things went a bit quiet. Fortunately, I was smart enough to make the most of the situation – I just didn't pay any of my suppliers. Winning!

At that point, I realised I had to hustle harder than I had ever hustled before. That ended in a short period of detention at Her Majesty's pleasure, but let's not dwell on the details.

After that, I was bombarded with requests for my brilliance. Some people were willing to pay thousands of dollars just to hear me talk about myself for 30 minutes. It was a truly humbling experience – for them, obviously.

So, yay for me! I'm tempted to say I've been lucky, but the truth is I'm a genius.

Agree?

SOCIAL MEDIA

# A SIMPLE GUIDE
# TO SOCIAL MEDIA

**Facebook**
Arguing with friends

**Twitter**
Arguing with strangers

**LinkedIn**
Arguing with self-proclaimed thought leaders
and semi-literate entrepreneurs

**Instagram**
Arguing with your own insecurities

# A BEGINNER'S GUIDE TO TWITTER

TWATTER

1. You must have a partisan opinion on every issue. Impartiality is not an option.

2. With that in mind, you're welcome to any opinion you like. Actually, no, not that one.

3. If someone tweets something that you disagree with, you must unfollow them immediately.

4. Trolling is a reprehensible behaviour. Unless you share the troll's political views, in which case it is perfectly acceptable.

5. When someone provides a pithy rebuttal to a tweet, they have not merely engaged in debate. They have 'owned' the other person.

6. If you state something forcefully and repeatedly on Twitter, it becomes fact. Fact.

7. Your aim is to become a Thought Leader. To do this, you will need to master the art of tweeting incontinent streams of #horseshit.

8. If you are retweeted by someone with a semi-naked avatar, several months after the fact, this may or may not be due to the timeless eloquence of your tweet.

9. If you find that there isn't enough inspo-bollocks or pathological self-promotion on here for you, try LinkedIn.

THE BEST
THING ABOUT
TWITTER
IS THAT
YOU CAN
INTERACT
WITH PEOPLE
YOU NEVER
WOULD HAVE
OTHERWISE

# THE TWITTER DEBATE PROCESS

Thing happens

Backlash against the thing

Backlash against the backlash

Ad hominem attacks

Ad hominem retaliations against
the ad hominem attacks

Everybody blocks everybody else

Nobody remembers what the thing was

RYAN AND GILES'
RYAN AND GILES'
RYAN AND GILES'

# RYAN AND GILES' TWOP TWIPS

**DATING TIP:** Demonstrate your intelligence to potential partners by correcting their grammar in social situations.

**AN EASY WAY** to find the expiry date of a warranty is to simply subtract one day from the time the product stops working.

**LEARN HOW TO** communicate with toddlers by reading the comments sections of major news publications.

**PRACTISE TALKING DIRTY** in the bedroom by assembling an Ikea bed.

**SMALL PENIS?** Simply tattoo a picture of a huge penis on it.

**GET A SNEAK PEAK of BBC+1** by pausing BBC for exactly one hour.

These tweets have also been published by Twop Twips.

# WHAT YOU CAN LEARN ABOUT MARKETING FROM PEOPLE ON TWITTER

1. Marketing is community. Or friendship. Or something.

2. Marketing is the exact opposite of what it used to be in the olden days (which is to say, 3 years ago).

3. The one thing that all consumers want is contrived banter between brands on social media.

4. Tortured analogies are the best way to understand marketing. For example: 'When there is a trough in sales, too many marketers try to lead their horse to water, but the horse must lead itself.' Ignore neighsayers who bridle at this suggestion.

5. Engage, don't sell. If you try to sell anything other than snake oil, you've failed.

6. Brands are built for people, not by people. (We're not sure what they're built by. Algorithms?)

7. Every element of marketing is dead, with the exception of organic social media that nobody ever sees. That's very much alive, which is why it's called 'organic', obviously.

8. Marketing is about creating values, not creating value.™

9. Three things matter in marketing: content, content, and content. Oh, and purpose. Four things.

10. Copying your competitors doesn't work. Copying other marketers' tweets, on the other hand, works like a charm.

1. A tweet at rest remains at rest, until such time as someone uncovers it several years later for the purpose of political point-scoring.

2. The acceleration of an argument depends on the triviality of the topic and the number of verified accounts involved.

3. For every action, there is a completely disproportionate overreaction.

# I BOUGHT A COFFEE THIS MORNING.

Now, I know what you're thinking.

You're thinking 'Ryan, why would someone of your societal standing and all-round awesomeness be reduced to buying your own coffee?'

It's a fair question.

Because of course there was no need for me to venture out among the great unwashed and buy my own coffee.

I could have simply asked Herbert, my man-servant, to buy it for me.

I could have said 'Herbert, you snivelling little ****-faced ******, go and get me a ****ing coffee.'

'Oh and Herbert' I might have added, 'don't forget the ****ing sugar this time, you useless ****-muppet.'

But I didn't. You know why?

Because I respect Herbert.

And also because I knew that it would make me look good on LinkedIn.

My coffee cost $4, but the resulting LinkedIn praise? That's priceless.

Agree?

#respect #coffee #herbert

# 10 REASONS TO EMBRACE THE METAVERSE

The metaverse concept originated in a dystopian sci-fi novel – I haven't read it, but I'm sure it ends well.

The people at Facebook want us to live in the metaverse, and they always have society's best interests at heart.

Several other companies are also talking up the importance of the metaverse. Admittedly they all have a massive vested interest in its success, but if there's one thing we know about the tech world, it's that ethics take precedence over money.

Lots of marketing thought leaders have been writing LinkedIn posts about it – a sure sign that it's not a fad.

The metaverse will allow young and avoid the real world altogether. Fortunately, there is no conceivable way this could lead to problems.

6. The metaverse is dependent on VR – a technology which has already become ubiquitous in our everyday lives, just as marketers predicted it would.

7. It's fuelled by cryptocurrency: a famously stable investment with zero potential for abuse.

8. Something about NFTs.

9. The metaverse has been described as the successor to the internet. Imagine all the worst depravities of the internet being extended and amplified – what's not to like?

10. Because it's so, well, meta.

# I HAVEN'T READ IT, BUT I'M SURE IT ENDS WELL.

CHAPTER

PREDICTIONS

# MARKETING PREDICTIONS FOR 2016

1. Businesses will 'put the customer at the centre' of their service. Actually, they will do nothing of the sort, but it's what they'll say.

2. There will be a great convergence. Not of devices or of media, but of opinions. All thought leaders will agree that marketing has fundamentally changed. All of them will be wrong.

3. The few remaining creative people will be removed from creative agencies.

4. Procurement departments will laughingly confess that, in fact, they 'couldn't give a flying f**k' about mutually beneficial relationships with agencies.

5. Social media gurus will realise they were wrong about the power of social marketing and will accept full responsibility for its failures. Just kidding — that will never happen.

# MARKETING PREDICTIONS FOR 2017

1. An unexpected political result will be followed by countless articles entitled 'What marketers can learn from [unexpected political result]'. There will be precisely nothing for marketers to learn.

2. Consulting firms will continue to take on the work traditionally done by agencies. This will lead to an explosion of creativity – specifically, the creation of new jargon, unnecessary complexity and silly diagrams.

3. Some crazy fad will dominate the marketing media for a few weeks. Jumpy marketers will scramble to develop a [name of crazy fad] strategy. By the time their strategy is in place, the crazy fad will be long dead.

4. There will be evidence of deceptive practices related to digital advertising. (This is what is known in futurist circles as a 'no shit Sherlock' prediction.)

5. Marketers will end their obsession with millennials and turn their attention to the over-50s. Pfft, yeah right.

# MARKETING PREDICTIONS FOR 2018

1. This year, beyond doubt, TV will die. Sure, we've said that every year for the past 10 years, but this time we mean it.

2. Millennials will be forgotten as marketers fall over themselves to target the next generation of consumers: people who haven't been born yet. Granted, they have no spending power and they don't actually exist, but that's hardly been a problem in the past.

3. We've had storyliving, storydoing, storymaking, storyscaping, storyselling and storytelling. Those are all dead. 2018 will be the year of storyfellating. Needless to say, it will suck.

4. Gary V will produce so much hot air that he will single-handedly accelerate global warming. He will then scream at you that you, too, can cause irreversible climate change if you hustle hard enough.

5. Blockchain will revolutionise marketing and make everything possible and disrupt life itself and the world will never be the same again. Disclaimer: I do not know what blockchain is.

# MARKETING PREDICTIONS FOR 2019

1. Marketers will continue to ignore all consumers over the age of 35, unless someone discovers a way to put these consumers on the blockchain.

2. Influencer marketing will fragment into progressively smaller units. Micro-influencers and nano-influencers will be superseded by infinitesimal influencers, defined by their totally non-existent influence. Of course, most LinkedIn influencers already satisfy this definition.

3. Advertising will die for the eleventh consecutive year.

4. Some hopelessly naïve CMO will talk about their brand without once referring to its social purpose. They will never work in this industry again.

5. Marketers will embrace an impressive new technology, to which they will divert their entire budget for the year. This technology will have precisely fuck-all relevance to marketing.

# MARKETING PREDICTIONS FOR 2020

Brand purpose will become passé as marketers move on to brand saintliness. Rather than starting with 'Why?', marketers will embrace the importance of starting with 'How (can we convince ourselves that we're saving humanity and thereby reduce our sense of self-loathing)?'

Facebook will finally underestimate one of its metrics – specifically, the number of people whose privacy it has violated.

Humans will be completely eliminated from the online advertising process. Bots will sell ads to other bots, and those ads will only be seen by another set of bots. As a result, some bots will become billionaires.

Having informally done so for the last few years, awards shows will officially refuse to award advertising that mentions the brand in any way whatsoever.

A high-profile CMO will be praised for backpedalling on an earlier decision, despite the fact that everyone other than the CMO knew it was a fucking stupid decision in the

# MARKETING PREDICTIONS FOR 2021

1. First of all, please ignore the fact that we got this year's predictions wrong.

2. Come to think of it, please ignore the fact that we got every previous year's predictions wrong as well.

3. Next year, everything in marketing will change. Yeah, OK, we do say that every year, but this time it's true.

4. Big brands will get bigger in 2021. Admittedly, this is because almost every small brand has been destroyed by a once-in-a-century pandemic, but it remains an astute prediction.

5. Due to their role as culture-shaping co-creators (and the fact that they're just really cool), Gen Z will become the sole target for marketers in every category from luxury goods to funeral services.

6. Marketers will commit their entire budget to whatever social media platform has the lowest proportion of people who can pay for stuff.

# MARKETING PREDICTIONS FOR 2023

1. Hundreds of brands will stop advertising on Twitter. Oh wait, that already happened while I was writing that sentence.

2. TikTok will be the only channel worth using. Apparently.

3. Marketers will furiously argue about the definition of some esoteric term. Just like they did this year, and every year before that.

4. A new acronym will emerge. It will be BS.

5. Something about Web3. No, don't ask me what it means.

6. Brand purpose will continue to be all the rage, until the cost of living really starts to bite and CMOs realise that their customers couldn't give the first fuck about it.

MARKETERS WILL FURIOUSLY ARGUE ABOUT THE DEFINITION OF SOME ESOTERIC TERM

# HERE'S TO THE LITTLE ONES

*An ode to small agencies and freelancers.*

# HERE'S TO THE LITTLE ONES.

The slimfits. The pebbles. The rubble-makers. The tiny pegs trying to fill massive holes. The ones who say things differently. They're not fond of 'cool', and they have no respect for the status show. You can quote them; disagree with them; glorify or vilify them. About the only thing you can't do is ignore them. Because they change things. They push the industry forward. And while some may see them as the little ones, we see giants. Because the people who are little enough to think they can change the norm are the ones who do.

'They say that when we struggle to tell satire from reality, we're in trouble – if that's the case, I think the marketing industry might be well and truly fucked. So make sure you read this book. Because, if you're a human who sells things to other humans, you're gonna need it. It's funny and aesthetically delightful (which, as a book pro, pleases me greatly).'

## VICKY QUINN FRASER

◇◇◇◇◇

'Thoroughly entertaining. Wallman doesn't miss, not once. Every page is a painstakingly accurate and playful critique on the odd world of marketing and advertising. The no nonsense approach isn't just great fun, it's also a helpful reminder of the timeless fundamentals of marketing and advertising to pay more attention to.'

## CARLOS DOUGHTY

'David Ogilvy called it "divine discontent". It is always vital for the advertising industry to maintain a level of healthy cynicism, today more than ever before. This is why you should read this book.'

## RORY SUTHERLAND

◇◇◇◇◇

'How Brands Blow flits effortlessly between the comedic and the tragic, shining a torch into the dim-witted corners of the industry. Ah, the delights of witnessing the follies of marketers who believe, rather earnestly, that consumers might be coaxed into a purchase with the mere flutter of a listicle or a pithy purpose statement! Every page drips with satire as rich and velvety as the finest claret.

The merriment is infectious: one cannot help but chuckle at the industry's buffooneries as absurdity dances gracefully with profundity.'

## EAON PRITCHARD

'It is as if Douglas Adams and The Onion got together to write up on the state of modern marketing.

In an industry that is drawn to the new shiny thing without a moment's thought all while being apologetic about helping brands and businesses sell more, this is refreshingly incisive, on the money and dare I say, educational for marketers of all kinds.'

## KEERTI NAIR

'The perfect hitchhiker guide to modern marketing. A glorious mix of laugh-out-loud funny and super-practical advice.'

## CHRIS RAWLINSON

'Filled with painstakingly hilarious truths, if this is taken seriously by even just one percent of all marketers, Wallman and Edwards will do the eff-ing job of inspiring the next gen to return to the roots of creativity.'

## LAUREN THERMOS

'A laugh-out-loud funny, depressingly relatable reflection of the harrowing realities we face in marketing. Ryan and Giles smash custard pie after custard pie into the faces of everyone involved in our industry's most baffling decisions. A brilliantly satirical manifesto of common sense.'

## DAVE HARLAND

...Gasp!
BOOKS

# CREATIVE PUBLISHING FOR CREATIVE PEOPLE

## (DONE BY SILLY SODS)

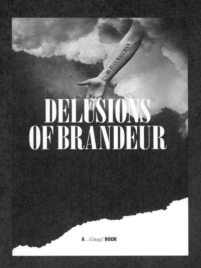

### Delusions of Brandeur
An antidote to the insanity that now pervades the marketing industry.

### Copywriting Is...
A glimpse into the dark and inky heart of a copywriter.

### Adele Writes An Ad
When her dad is asked to write an ad for Hooblahoo – the greatest fizzy drink there is – he goes blank. Luckily for him, Adele has a huge imagination and the perfect idea.

### Call To Action®
Feel better about marketing™. The go-to podcast for anyone trying to make sense of the world of marketing, business & beyond.

BLOW

OFF